33
USEFUL PROJECTS
FOR THE
WOODWORKER

BY SCHOOL SHOP
MAGAZINE

TAB BOOKS Inc.
Blue Ridge Summit, PA 17214

TAB BOOKS Inc. offers software for sale. For information and a catalog, please contact TAB Software Department, Blue Ridge Summit, PA 17294-0850.

FIRST EDITION
SECOND PRINTING

Printed in the United States of America

Library of Congress Cataloging in Publication Data

33 useful projects for the woodworker.

Includes index.
1. Woodwork. I. School shop. II. Title: Thirty-three useful projects for the woodworker.
TT180.A11   1986   684'.08   86-23154

ISBN 0-8306-0783-8
ISBN 0-8306-2783-9 (pbk.)

Questions regarding the content of this book should be addressed to:

Reader Inquiry Branch
Editorial Department
TAB BOOKS Inc.
P.O. Box 40
Blue Ridge Summit, PA 17214

Contents

Part Three   87
Projects Using Special Techniques and Tools

Part Four   117
Projects with Special Additions

Part Five   131
Finishes and Finishing

Index   152

Introduction

The projects here are for woodworkers of all skill levels. The beginner and advanced woodworker alike will find a challenge, and will probably learn something new. The projects include home furnishings, useful shop equipment, items for outside use, and even something for the kids.

The book is organized such that Part One provides some instruction woodworkers might want to read up on—whether they are experienced or not. Parts Two, Three, and Four include the actual projects. Part Five explains how to finish the projects.

There is much room for creativity. By using the various tools available, different types of wood, materials other than wood—and your imagination—the possibilities are endless. As you gain skills, the basic plans provided here can be altered to meet your needs.

All of the outstanding projects in this book have been made available by the editors of *School Shop* magazine, the how-to-do-it publication that has printed articles relating to industrial and technical education since 1941. Without their efforts and cooperation, this book would not be possible.

Part One

Before Starting—
Some Helpful Tips

This section contains some information you might want to have before starting woodworking projects. Warpage, for example, is always a problem, and understanding moisture control will help you avoid the pitfalls. You will get an idea as to what a general shop should be equipped with, how you can keep wood cost down, and interesting insight to designing and laminating projects.

Understanding Moisture Control

Most woodworkers have encountered problems with wood warpage. Here are some hints to help you avoid the problem.

* * *

The dimensional stability of the wood you will be using is a major problem. Many woodworkers have been frustrated by projects that warp or crack, and by lumber that seems to twist overnight. There is little most of us can do about these common problems except to try to understand the causes and conditions of these changes and accept them as compromises we must make when working with one of nature's most useful products.

Wood's dimensional stability problems are due to its hydroscopic nature and our lack of control over the laboratory environment. As a hydroscopic material, wood gains or loses water in direct relationship to its environment. These changes in moisture content produce shrinkage or swelling, which causes problems.

If the moisture and temperature environment could be controlled as wood is shipped, stored, worked with, and finally used, we would have few problems. We cannot, however, usually do this.

MOISTURE CONTENT

Green lumber may contain a moisture content of from 30 to 300 percent. For all practical purposes, dimensional stability is only affected below the wood fiber's saturation point, which is usually about 28 percent. Shrinkage or swelling can be considered to be roughly proportional to moisture content changes below the fiber saturation point.

The amount of shrinkage or swelling that takes place between 30 and zero percent ranges from approximately 3.5 to 15 percent, tangential direction, down to .1 to .9 percent, longitudinal direction. Depending on the species, our lumber supplies could shrink up to about .5 percent across the grain for every percent change in moisture content.

Wood in storage, if given time, will attain a moisture equilibrium with its atmospheric moisture content. This equilibrium is not an equality in that 90 percent relative humidity will create 90 percent wood moisture content, but a specific relationship does exist. There are many charts and tables available that can be used to determine wood's equilibrium moisture content for given relative humidities and temperatures.

If, for example, you purchase your lumber supply in summer and store it in a room that reaches 85 degrees Fahrenheit and relative humidity of at least 80 percent, kiln dried lumber will equalize, if given time, at about 15.7 percent moisture content. If, then, when colder weather comes, and humidity is lowered to 25 percent at 70 degrees, our lumber will equalize at about 5.5 percent.

With this data, we can predict what can happen to our lumber. The moisture content can change up to 10 percent, and if we have up to .5 percent shrinkage across the grain for every percent change, we get a 5 percent change in size. This equals up to 1/2 inch for every 10 inches of width, dependent upon the species.

CONTROLLING CHANGES

While we can't eliminate shrinkage and swelling, we can ease it by maintaining a constant moisture content, or by using polyethylene glycol for stabilization.

Probably the best procedure is to use construction methods that allow for some shrinkage and swelling without damage to the article. These include floating panels, fastening methods that

Cracked, warped lumber, resulting from improper moisture control, is a constant woodworking problem.

allow movement, grain orientations so unequal movement across and along the grain does not conflict, and using relatively stable materials in areas where wide panels are needed and solid wood is not essential. Some of the most easily used materials are plywood, hardboard, particleboard, and flake board. These materials are considerably more stable than most solid woods and are extensively used in the wood products industries. Today's furniture makes extensive use of these materials for applications such as hardwood veneer plywood sides, cabinet doors, backs, dust panels, and drawer parts.

Board selection for critical parts of projects can minimize warping. If quarter-sawn boards are used, or if wide boards are ripped and reglued with the annual ring direction of every other piece reversed, warpage—but not shrinkage—is reduced.

These partial solutions can be expanded upon. Perhaps the most important factor, however, is an awareness of the causes and extent of dimensional instability in wood that allows us to be tolerant and work with and not against natural characteristics.

Beat the High High Cost
of Walnut Turning Blocks

Walnut wood is great to work with and makes a fine finished product. It is, however, an expensive wood. Here is a way to cut costs and still use walnut.

* * *

If you are looking for high-quality walnut wood for turning bowls, vases, round platters, and similar projects, think in terms of walnut log cross-sections.

These particular cross-sections are sawn from green logs, debarked and rounded on a lathe, and stabilized at high temperature with polyethylene glycol-1000 (PEG) to prevent splitting and checking, and then kiln-dried to 6 percent moisture content. The material is free of seasoning degrade, and will stay that way.

The round bolts produce beautiful bowls with a distinctive grain pattern—somewhat comparable to rotary-cut veneer—not otherwise attainable.

PEG treatment, followed by thorough drying, is the key to successful use of this material. Log and limb cross-sections normally check badly and develop typical pie-shaped cracks during the drying process. This is because wood shrinks twice as much in the tangential plane (roughly parallel to the growth rings) as in the radial direction.

The internal stresses that result from such differential shrinkage are tremendous. Invariably they cause serious checks and splits as the wood loses moisture down to equilibrium moisture content (about 6 percent) in the rather arid environment of a heated or air-conditioned woodshop. PEG treatment, which physically bulks the wood fibers, largely prevents shrinkage, and thus prevents the development of destructive stresses.

ECONOMY IS GOOD NEWS

For budget-conscious woodworkers, the relative economy of the treated material is good news in today's economy, when escalating prices of thick blocks of kiln-dried walnut suitable for turning reflect the diminishing supply of trees, the continued strong demand for this fine hardwood, and the ever-rising costs of logging, sawmilling, kiln-drying, and related processing.

When buying this material, note that in all instances the round bolts cost less than comparable square blocks, the price advantage ranging from 1 to 5 percent in the smaller sizes to

29 percent in some of the larger sizes. All sizes considered, the average savings is 15 percent.

WASTE IS EXPENSIVE

The main reason for the price differential is that with a square block, 12- x -12- x -4 inches, 22 percent of the material is wasted in preparing the block for turning. This is needless waste of a valuable natural resource that is in short supply and that costs more than 0.7 cents per cubic inch net scale in the standing tree.

Much better and more complete use of the resource, together with even greater financial savings, is possible if you are in a walnut-producing area. Commercial loggers of walnut timber normally leave in the woods to rot relatively large volumes of usable material in the form of unwanted limbs and odd-shaped bolts that are too short or too small in diameter for efficient processing. Sawmills also generate quite a bit of residue potentially usable for woodshop projects. Usually this waste can be had for the asking. State foresters or county agricultural agents can often direct you to active logging and sawmilling operations in rural areas.

The large walnut planter and the vases in the illustration can be made from this class of round "waste" material. Because of their height (10 inches), it is not feasible to process them like smaller bowls; that is, from pretreated dry bolts. The reason is that the practical effective depth of PEG diffusion into walnut end grain is about 2 inches. This limits the thickness of prestabilized

Walnut log cross sections.

Bowls from dry, stabilized crosssections up to 4 inches thick, and planters and vases form green bolts 12 inches long.

walnut turning bolts to approximately 4 inches.

A slightly different technique is used in processing the planter and vase. Cylindrical holes 8 inches deep and 6 inches in diameter for the planter (3 inches in diameter for the vase) are drilled into rounded green bolts of suitable length and diameter. The partially hollowed-out bolts are placed on a lathe and shaped to the desired exterior configuration. They are soaked for an appropriate period in a 50 percent solution of PEG-1000, dried, sanded, finished with a Danish oil especially formulated for use on treated wood, waxed, and polished. They are just as free of seasoning degrade (checks, splits, etc.) as are bowls made from prestabilized bolts up to 4 inches thick.

Laminating and
Designing Wood Projects

Introduce a new dimension to your woodworking by laminating the wood yourself.

* * *

European countries, particularly Switzerland, Sweden, and Germany—and the United States—have been producing glued, laminated forms for quite a few years. Many such forms were observed in 1936 during a European trip by a staff member of the United States Forest Products Laboratory, Madison, Wisconsin.[1]

Plywood is a laminate produced by bonding at least two layers of wood with their grains running at 90-degree angles to each other. Most plywood, however, is a flat sandwich, and the flatness does not represent an essential feature of a laminate. Wood veneers, usually available in thicknesses of 1/16 inch and 1/28 inch, are flexible both with and across the grain. Such veneers are capable, singly and stacked, of being bent to conform to a surface that has a marked curvature. In fact, with sufficient pressure, it is possible to produce a laminate having a compound curve.

In hardwood plywood—walnut, for example—the two outer layers are relatively thin veneers of walnut, if it is classed as "good two sides," or walnut and some other hardwood if it is classed as "good one side." The inner layer contributes almost three-quarters of the thickness and is constructed of basswood, yellow poplar, or some other less-expensive wood. In such panels, as in most plywood, the layers are not all the same thickness nor are they all the same variety or quality of wood. But even these two characteristics are not always found in laminates, since it is sometimes best to use the same wood all the way through and to use veneers of the same thickness in producing a laminated section.

And so, to the craftsman, a laminate becomes a section of stock, flat or curved, that is constructed by sandwiching veneers and bonding them under pressure, using an adhesive. There are no restrictions concerning direction of grain, thickness of layers, or variety of wood. The only determiner of technique is the design of the project. Parenthetically, it might be added that there are many suitable adhesives available. Vegetable glue, urea resin, casein glue, and blood albumin glue are used commercially in

9

the manufacture of plywood and laminates. The craftsman is likely to find that a high-quality urea resin or water-resistant casein glue works best. Animal and fish glues lack water resistance, and polyvinyl resin, in addition to being low in water resistance, sets too rapidly and is flexible enough to permit "creep" under certain conditions.

PRODUCING THE FORM

The first step in producing a laminated project is to design the project. Full-size patterns of all curves must be drawn. The edge curve of the project is then traced in the same direction as the grain on the edge of a block of maple, birch, or other hardwood. The block must have enough width and length to permit the lamination of a piece large enough to allow the top view of the project to be traced on the rough laminate. The thickness of the block depends somewhat on the desired thickness of the laminate and to a greater extent on the width and length of the project. In general, the thicker, wider, and longer the laminate desired, the thicker the block should be; and a good rule to follow is to select a block thickness that will provide *at least* 1 1/2 inches of material on each side of the edge curve at all points along the curve. In addition, it is often necessary to drill several edge-to-edge holes through the block at points along the curve where the thickness of block between the curve and the face of the block is 2 inches or less, and drive dowel pins through the block as in the illustration. The pins strengthen the form greatly and guard against failure or deflection during the laminating process.

The next step is to saw the edge curve using a bandsaw equipped with a blade narrow enough to permit following the curve accurately. It is important to perform this operation carefully. The laminating process is sufficiently sensitive to show sawing irregularities. Moreover, the two parts of the block, after sawing, represent the male and female parts of the laminating form, and the contact between the two is nearly perfect. Sanding or filing to remove saw irregularities destroys the contact and produces ultimately a laminate of uneven thickness.

Each of the curved surfaces of the two parts of the form must be lined with a material that tends to smooth out small irregularities caused by sawing. The lining material used must be one to which glue does not adhere well. The rubber used in the manufacture of automobile inner tubes has been found to be satisfactory. It is heavy enough to provide an adequate cushion, but it will not bond to the laminate, especially if the rubber is polished with paste wax occasionally. The rubber liner can be stapled in place or fastened with wire nails that have small, flat heads. Whichever method is used, fasteners should be driven far enough into the rubber so that they cannot imprint themselves in the laminate. Seams in the rubber should be sanded flat. The rubber liner on each part of the form, and the sides of the form, should be covered with waxed paper to allow the form to part easily when the lamination is complete.

THE ROUGH LAMINATE

Enough veneers to provide the desired final thickness should be selected, and each veneer (except the outer two which will be coated on one side only) should be coated with glue on both sides. The veneers are then stacked and placed between the two parts of the form, and pressure is applied to the flat faces of the form, as in the illustration. Depending on the size of the laminate, pressure may be applied with C-clamps (tightened carefully with a wrench), bar or pipe clamps, a vise, a press of some kind, or any combination of these. The laminate should be kept under pressure for a minimum of 24 hours.

FINAL STEPS

Following removal from the form, the top view of the project is traced on the laminate, and the project is cut out, shaped, smoothed, and finished. A mark should be filed at the edge of the form at one end or the other to mark the point at which the top view pattern should be placed on the laminate to obtain the proper portion of the curve in the project.

Very soon after removing the rough laminate from the form, the project should be brought to the finishing stage and thoroughly sealed. A laminate is under internal stress at all times and, like solid wood, reacts to humidity, though to a decidedly lesser degree than solid wood. Trimming away excess stock and finishing seems to decrease greatly any tendency for distortion to appear. Even so, some designs need additional support, and glue blocks, nails, and stiffeners of various kinds are used occasionally to help maintain laminated curves.

Greater strength across the grain of a laminate can be achieved by changing by 90 degrees the direction of the grain of each succeeding layer. Such a technique also helps to control distortion after the piece is removed from the form. It does not, however, eliminate the tendency toward distortion. Where a piece is to be sculptured after lamination, the best appearance is most often obtained by placing the veneers so that all grain runs in the same direction.

CONCLUSION

In the final analysis, lamination is important commercially and to the individual craftsman because of the design possibilities it offers. A laminated piece is considerably stronger, harder, longer wearing, and less subject to failure than a piece of solid wood having the same dimensions. Lamination permits designs that are lighter in weight but exceptionally strong. It is also a process that is very much less wasteful of wood than production from solid stock, because little wood is wasted in cutting a log into veneer, and the laminate trimmings are usually small. As such, the process of lamination helps us to improve an important natural product without sacrificing its inherent beauty and without undue waste.

The individual craftsman will find the possibilities fascinating.

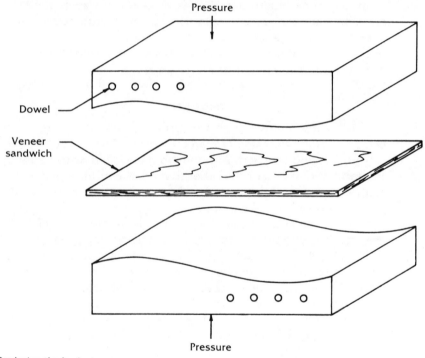

Producing the laminate.

PROCEDURE FOR SALAD SERVERS

1. Complete the design. Accurately drawn full-sized patterns of the piece are needed as are specifications concerning the kind and thickness of veneer, number of layers needed, type of glue to be used, sculpturing to be done on the rough laminate, and the type of finish to be used.

(The set is made of six layers of 1/28-inch walnut veneer, stacked so the grain runs in one direction, glued with urea resin glue, and finished using the Sealacell process.)

2. Produce the wood form. Be sure that the form is strong enough to withstand the pressure that will be applied and that the curved faces of the form are properly lined with rubber and wax paper. The form should be somewhat greater in width and length than the finished piece is to be.

3. Cut a sufficient number of pieces of veneer to approximately the width of the form. Each piece should be as long as the curved faces of the form.

4. Produce the rough laminate. Allow a glue drying time of at least 24 hours before removing the rough laminate from the form.

5. Trace the shape of the top view on the rough laminate, saw it out and complete the sculpturing, smoothing, and finishing operations. This step should be completed as soon as the rough laminate has been removed from the form so that distortion will be minimized.

Equipping Your Shop

Following is a list of tools, machines, and equipment for a general woodworking shop. Every woodworker, of course, will require different things depending on the project, but here you can get an idea (especially if you're a novice) as to what to start collecting!

* * *

HAND TOOLS

Item	Quantity
Awl, scratch, 6 inches overall length	2
Bits, auger, No. 4 to 16 by 16ths, set	1
Bits, countersink, rosehead, 5/8 inch	2
Bits, dowel, 1/4 inch	1
Bits, dowel, 3/8 inch	1
Bits, Forstner, 1/4 inch	1
Bits, Forstner, 3/8 inch	1
Bits, Forstner, 1/2 inch	1
Bits, screwdriver, forged steel, 1/4 inch and 3/8 inch	1
Bit, expansive, forged steel, 2 interchangeable cutters, range from 7/8 inch to 3 inches	1
Bit, brace, ratchet, 10 inches, universal jaw	2
Bit, gage, 1 inch capacity, double-set-screw type	2
Brushes, glue, 1 inch x 5/8 inch, oval type	2
Brushes, paint, 2 inches, medium grade	5
Brushes, paint, 1 1/2 inches, medium grade	3
Brushes, paint, 1 inch, medium grade	2
Brushes, wire, 1 inch x 5 inch block, overall length 10 inches	2
Burnisher, oval blade, 4 1/2 inch blade, overall 7 1/2 inches	1
Calipers, inside, spring type, solid nut, 6 inches	1
Calipers, outside, spring type, solid nut, 6 inches	1
Card and brush, file, brush, 1 1/2 inches by 5 inches, 9 inches overall length	2
Carving knife, Sloyd type, 3 1/8 inch blade	2
Carving tool set, consisting of 5/16 inch straight chisel, 3/8 inch bent gouge, 3/8 inch bent chisel, 1/4 inch skew chisel, 3/32 inch veining tool	1
Chisels, wood, butt type, 1/4 inch	1
Chisels, wood, butt type, 3/8 inch	1
Chisels, wood, butt type, 1/2 inch	1
Chisels, wood, butt type, 3/4 inch	1

Chisels, wood, butt type, 1 inch 1
Clamps, C, steel screw, malleable iron frame, 6 inches .. 6
Clamps, I-bar, carbon steel, acme threaded, 36 inches ... 4
Clamps, I-bar, carbon steel, acme threaded, 48 inches ... 4
Clamps, I-bar, carbon steel, acme threaded, 72 inches ... 4
Combination square set, 12 inch steel rule graduated to 1/64
    inch, complete less protractor 1
Compass, pencil, 6 inches, solid nut adjustment 2
Dividers, 6 inches, solid nut adjustment, polished 2
Dowel sharpener, tapered steel shank 1
Doweling jig, 3 inch capacity, complete with 3/16 inch, 1/4
    inch, 5/16 inch, 3/8 inch, 7/16 inch, 1/2 inch guides 1
Drawing knife, hollow ground 10 inches x 1 3/8 inch steel
    blade 1
Duster, bench, 8 inch brush, 13 inch length 12
Dresser, grinding wheel, complete with two sets of cutters 1
Drill, electric, 1/4 inch capacity, 110-220, ac, 1,100 rpm . 1
Drill, hand, 1/4 inch capacity, with drive and idler pinion,
    10 1/2 inches overall length 1
Drill, twist, straight shank, carbon steel, 1/16 inch 6
Drill, twist, straight shank, carbon steel, 3/32 inch 6
Drill, twist, straight shank, carbon steel, 1/8 inch 6
Drill, twist, straight shank, carbon steel, 5/32 inch 6
Drill, twist, straight shank, carbon steel, 3/16 inch 6
Drill, twist, straight shank, carbon steel, 7/32 inch 6
Drill, twist, straight shank, carbon steel, 1/4 inch 3
Drill, twist, straight shank, carbon steel, 5/16 inch 3
Drill, twist, straight shank, carbon steel, 3/8 inch 3
Drill, twist, straight shank, carbon steel, 7/16 inch 1
Drill, twist, straight shank, carbon steel, 1/2 inch 1
File, auger bit, 7 inches, one flat, one triangular end 2
File, flat mill, bastard cut, 10 inches 4
File, half-round, 10 inches, double cut, bastard 2
File, square, wood, double cut, bastard, 8 inches 2
File, three square, wood, double cut, bastard, 6 inches .. 2
File, round, wood, 8 inches 1
Gage, marking, mortise 2
Glass cutter, turret head 1
Goggles, safety, shatter-proof, replaceable lens type 1
Gouge, handled, paring, leather tipped, 1/4 inch 1
Gouge, handled, paring, leather tipped, 1/2 inch 1
Gouge, handled, paring, leather tipped, 3/4 inch 1
Hack saw, adjustable frame, pistol grip 1
Hack-saw blades, 10 inches, medium tooth 12
Hammer, nail, 13 ounces, curved claw, bell face, polished
    face and claw 2

Hand screws, adjustable, maple jaws, steel spindles, No. 1, 6 inch opening 4

Hand screws, adjustable, maple jaws, steel spindles, No. 3, 10 inch opening 4

Hand screws, adjustable, maple jaws, steel spindles, No. 2, 8 1/2 inch opening 4

Hand screws, adjustable, maple jaws, steel spindles, No. 4, 12 inch opening 2

Heater, glue, 1 quart capacity, electrical, thermostatic heat control, removable pot, complete with cord and plug   1

Hammer, nail, 16 ounce curved claw, bell face, polished face and claw 2

Hammer, upholsterer's magnetic, 7 ounces, polished 1

Mallets, hickory, 3 inches × 5 inches, complete with handle   2

Nail sets, square head, polished, one each 1/32 inch, 2/32 inch, and 3/32 inch points 3

Oilstone, crystolon, or similar combination, 2 inches × 7 inches × 1 inch 2

Oilstone, slip, India, round edges, 1 3/4 inches × 4 1/2 inches 1

Plane, block, 6 inch length, 1 5/8 inch low-angle cutter, end and side adjustments, nickel trimming 2

Plane, jack, 14 inch overall length, 2 inch cutter, wood knob and handle, smooth bottom 12

Pliers, combination, 6 inches, machined, oil tempered, forged steel 2

Punch, center, 3/8 inch stock, 5 inch length 1

Putty knife, 1 1/4 inches, flexible steel blade, 7 inch overall length 1

Rules, bench, 12 inches × 1 1/8 inches, maple with brass tips   6

Rules, bench, 24 inches × 1 1/4 inches, maple with brass tips   2

Rule, zig-zag, folding, 6 feet, white finish 1

Saw, back, 12 inches, 15 point, tempered steel blade, polished back 4

Saw, compass, 12 inches, reversible tempered steel blade   1

Saw, coping, spring steel frame, wood handle, for 6 1/2 inch pin blades 6

Saw, cross cut, 22 inches, 10 point, straight back, taper ground, polished 3

Saw, rip, 26 inches, 5 1/2 inch point, straight back, taper ground, polished 1

Scraper, cabinet, 3 inches × 5 inches 4

Scraper, cabinet, 2 3/4 inch cutter, 11 inches overall, cast-iron frame with raised handles 1

Screwdriver, 2 1/2 inch blade through handle 2

Screwdriver, 4 inch blade through handle 2

Screwdriver, 6 inch blade through handle 2
Screwdriver, 3 inch Phillips 1
Screwdriver, 4 inch Phillips 1
Spokeshave, 1 3/4 inch cutter, cast-iron frame, 9 inches
    overall length, raised handles 2
Square, framing, one-piece steel, body 24 inches x 2
    inches, tongue 16 inches x 1 1/2 inches 1
Square, sliding "T" bevel, 8 inch steel blade, brass tipped
    handle 1
Square, try, 8 inch steel blade, brass face plate on wood
    handle 12
Wrecking bar, goose-neck, 24 inches overall 1
Wrench, crescent, standard, 6 inches, 3/4 inch capacity . 1
Wrench, crescent standard, 8 inches, 15/16 inch capacity 1
Wrench, crescent standard, 10 inches, 1 1/8 inch capacity 1

SHOP FURNITURE

Bench, woodworking, 4-place locker type, 54 inch x 64 inch
    bench surface, 2 1/4 inch thick maple top equipped with
    4 vises, 12 lockers or drawers in base 3
Bookcase, four-shelf enclosed type 1
Cabinet, filing, 15 inches wide, 28 inches deep, 4-drawer 1
Cabinet, tool (material to make in shop) 1
Chairs and stools (A suitable chair should be provided for
    the instructor and sufficient stools or folding chairs for
    students so that all members of the class can be seated
    when so desired.) . . . .
Desk, instructor's, 30 inches x 48 inches flat top with
    drawers 1
Fire extinguisher, vaporizing liquid type, 1 quart capacity 2
First-aid kit 1
Panel, tool (Material to make in shop) 2
Table, drawing and planning, 30 inches x 60 inches top 2
Table, glue and finish, 24 inches x 60 inches, metal covered
    top, 1 shelf 1

POWER-TOOL SPECIFICATIONS

Grinder—1/3 hp, ball bearing, 6 inches x 3/4 inch wheels; com-
    plete with wheels, wheel guards, eye shields, tool rests,
    stand, water pot, switch, cord and attachment plug . 1
Circular saw—10 inch floor model, tilting arbor, minimum table
    22 inches x 25 inches, quick positioning rip fence with ver-
    nier final adjustment; mitre gage with stop rods, safety

guards and splitter, complete with one 10 inch combination blade; 1-hp, 110-220-v, 60-c, a-c., ball-bearing motor, motor pulley, belt, cord, switch, and plug 1

Jig saw—24 inch capacity, four speed, 1/3-hp, 1725-rpm., 110-v, a-c motor; complete with stands, pulleys, belt, belt guard, light switch, cord, and plug 1

Drill press—14 inches or 15 inches, floor model, 2 3/4 inch ground steel column; Jacobs key-type chuck, 1/2 inch capacity; mortising attachments, complete with 1/4 inch, 3/8 inch, 1/2 inch hollow chisels and hollow chisel bits; 1/3-hp, 1725-rpm, 60-c, 110-v, single-phase, ball-bearing motor; complete with pulleys, belts, switch cord, and plug . . 1

Lathe, wood—12 inch swing, 38 inches between centers, cast-iron bed, 4-step "V" pulleys on headstock and motor, speed range 900 to 3400 rpm; headstock pulley and belt fully guarded, spindle 1 inch diameter or larger, threaded for inboard and out-board turning; No. 2 Morse tapers for centers, tailstock center self-ejecting; 1/2-hp, 1725-rpm, 110-220-v, 60-c, a-c motor. Complete with stand, pulleys, belt, spur center, cup center, 6 inch face plate, 3 inch face plate, 12 inch tool rest, 4 inch tool rest, cord, switch and plug; one set of turning chisels, one each 1 inch skew, 1/2 inch skew, 3/4 inch gouge, 1/4 inch gouge, 1/2 inch spear, 1/2 inch parting tool, and 1/2 inch round-nose tool 1

Router shaper—1/2-hp, 18,000 rpm, 110-v, a-c power unit; complete with base, chuck, guides, cord, switch and plug; cutters to include 1/8 inch veining bit, 1/4 inch router bit, 1/4 inch radius beading bit, 3/8 inch radius cove bit 1

Jointer—6 inch floor model or mounted on enclosed cast iron stand with chute. "V" belt drive, 37 inches overall length, round three-knife cutter head, sealed ball bearings, rapid action fence, cutter head guard and belt pulley guard, 1/2-hp, 110-220-v, 60-c, ball-bearing motor, pulleys, belts, switch, cord and knives 1

Sander—portable belt type, minimum 1/4 hp, universal dc-ac 25-60 c, single phase, 110 or 220-v; rubber covered drive pulley, ball bearings; with dust bag, complete with cord, switch, and plug 1

Band saw—14 inch single piece cast-iron frame; table tilt 45 degrees, grooved for mitre gage, 16 inches × 16 inches table top; capacity guide to table, 9 inches, capacity blade to frame, 14 inches; balanced, rubber-covered, ball-bearing wheels; adjustable guard and guides; 1/2-hp, single-phase, 1725-rpm, a-c, 60-c, 110-220-v motor; complete with belt guard, motor bracket, base or stand, two 3/8 inch blades, cord, switch, and plug 1

STATIONARY POWER TOOLS

Saw, circular, 10 inches, tilting arbor, with accessories and
    safety attachments 1
Saw, band, 20 inches, metal-wood cutting, variable speed   1
Saw, radial, 10 inches, with miter, bevel, and cutoff scales   1
Saw, jig, 24 inches, with adjustable table and blower . . .   1
Drill press, 20 inches, floor model 1
Lathe, wood, 12 inches × 36 inches capacity 1
Lathe, bow, 16 inch capacity (for large face plate turning)   1
Sander, belt and disc, floor model, with tilting table 1
Sander, belt, hand-stroke type, 6 inches × 14 feet 1 inch belt   1
Planer, 12 inch × 4 inch capacity 1
Jointer, 8 inches 1
Grinder, pedestal type, 6 inches 1

PORTABLE POWER TOOLS

Drill, electric, 1/2 inch 1
Drill, electric, 1/4 inch 1
Drill, compact, 1/4 inch, with right angle head 1
Sander, belt, 3 inches × 27 inches (belt size) 1
Sander, orbital-finishing 1
Saw, jig 1
Saw, circular (skill) 1
Router, complete kit 1
Shaper, hand 1

Part Two
Wood Projects

In this section you will find projects involving beginning through advanced skill levels. The projects require working with various hand and power tools, and different kinds of woods.

1: Match Holder

Use this simple project to start yourself out in woodworking. It is also a project for young woodworkers.

* * *

This hexagon-shaped match holder, besides being a striking piece of mantle decor, also serves as a practice woodworking project. The holder pictured was fashioned from walnut, to complement a walnut mantle. Colorful 11-inch fireplace matches to fill the container are easily obtained.

For machining purposes, the stock was first cut to a rough length of 17 3/4 inches. Prior to gluing, the pieces were cut to lengths of 8 7/8 inches. The base is made from 1/2-inch stock cut to fit 1/4 inch into the hexagon sides. Lacquer sealer and lacquer were used to finish the piece.

Finished match holder.

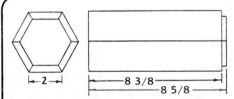

├─2─┤   ├────8 3/8────┤
        ├────8 5/8────┤

Procedure

1. Select stock
2. Cut to rough length, 17 3/4"
3. Plane stock to 3/8" (1" rough stock may be resawed)
4. Joint one edge
5. Rip stock to 2" widths
6. Set jointer fence at 30° and joint pieces*
7. Cut to rough length of 8 7/8"

8. Glue up sides, use rubber bands for clamps
9. When dry, remove rubber bands
10. Square ends on table saw or band saw
11. Cut bottom from 1/2" stock
12. Glue in bottom
13. When dry, sand project
14. Finish

*The 3/8" stock is jointed at 60° by setting the jointer fence on a 30° angle because the jointer fence is graduated from the vertical.

Measurements and procedure for match holder.

2: Cutting Board

This attractive and useful project is a good one for beginners to practice basic skills.

* * *

PROCEDURE

1. Select two different kinds of wood, preferably of contrasting colors: pine and mahogany, walnut and maple, etc.
2. Use boards of equal size (9 inches × 12 inches × 3/4 inch) to fit most standard wood vises.
3. Place one board on top of the other and fasten with 1 1/2-inch nails along the edges.
4. Draw a freeform design and cut out the shapes on the band saw.
5. Remove the nails and interchange the shapes.
6. Glue the edges of the pieces with waterproof white glue,

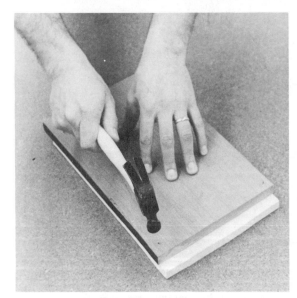

Mark freeform design and cut on band saw.

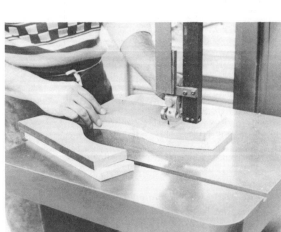

Nail together boards of equal size and contrasting color.

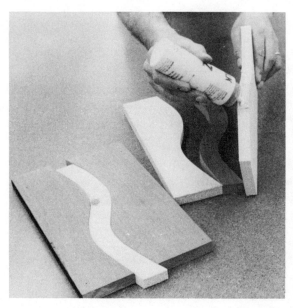

Apply non-toxic mineral oil finish.

Separate boards, interchange pieces, and glue and clamp the work.

following directions on the glue bottle, and clamp or secure the work until the glue sets.

7. Put the cutting board through the surfacer to complete the first stage of smoothing the work.

8. Using a compass and dividers, draw an outline of the finished piece and cut along the penciled line on the band saw.

9. Complete the cutting board by routing the edges, or hand finish it with a file and sanding block.

10. Drill a hole in the handle and add leather lacing to hang. Complete the sanding by hand, using 80, 120, and 220 grit paper. Hand rub finish the board with mineral oil (non-toxic).

11. At home, use only one side for cutting, hang up the board with the good side showing.

3: Spice Rack

Are you looking for a product that is well designed?. . . that incorporates many basic hand-tool and machine operations?. . . that displays a good selection of woods and yet is inexpensive to produce? Here is a project that will teach valuable skills and prove a useful item for home or gift-giving.

* * *

Walnut, which has the desired strength and density to make it suitable for use on the lathe, was selected as the basic raw material, with pine chosen for the dowel rods to provide contrast in wood textures. The natural beauty of walnut, of course, insures the attractiveness of the finished product.

Because the intended product will be used in the kitchen or on the dining table, we decided on a mineral-oil finish. This requires smoothly-sanded surfaces, but it is easy to apply and to clean. The oil further enhances the warm richness of the wood.

All joints are easy to construct and are generally of the butt-type. Dowel rods fit into drilled holes in both sections. A standard moisture-proof glue was used on all joints.

Dimensions and overall size are important because of the nature of the product and the desired proportions. The set was designed specifically to avoid simplicity. By calling for a suspension of the shakers from holders, the project becomes more challenging by reason of the expanded number of handtool and machine operations it entails.

The holders are offset to stimulate visual interest and to readily distinguish the salt from the pepper. The rack has been designed to set on the table or to hang on a wall or cabinet.

The set is easily cleaned by wiping off with a damp cloth and should last a considerable time with reasonable care.

Materials

Part	Material	Quant.	Finish Size
Shaker	Walnut	2	2" x 2" x 5"
Back	Walnut	1	1/4" x 1" x 7"
Rack	Walnut	2	1/4" x 4 1/8" d
Base	Walnut	1	1/4" x 4 1/8" d
Dowel	Pine	2	1/4" d x 6 1/2"

Materials list for spice rack.

PROCEDURE

Shakers

1. Cut two 2-x-2-x-5-inch pieces on a radial arm saw or by hand. Be certain ends are square. Always follow safety rules when operating power equipment and wear eye protection.
2. Place stock on lathe. Begin to turn down to correct size, but leave about 1/8-inch oversized diameter to allow for sanding.
3. Cut a notch 1/4 inch wide × 3/16 inch deep in given location.
4. Cut off stock at ends to about 1/2 inch. Clamp securely in vise. Cut off excess wood.
5. Hand sand ends (top and bottom) so that they are smooth and flat. Do any other finish sanding that might be necessary.
6. Again check that work is held tightly in vise. Drill a 1/2-inch hole 3 inches deep and a 3/4-inch counterbore 3/16 inch deep.
7. Drill holes in tops, and as indicated in drawing.

Holders

1. Cut bottom section out of 1/4-inch stock about 4 1/2 inches in diameter with a 2-inch flat side using a power jig saw or coping saw.
2. Cut a notch 1/4 inch deep and 1 inch wide, slightly undersized, along the center of flat edge with a coping saw. Clean with a file and/or sandpaper.
3. Follow the same procedure for upper holder section, but with a 3 1/2-inch diameter and a flat edge 1 1/2 inches long. Be sure that work is held firmly in vise.
4. Cut out large rounded notches for shakers with coping saw or power jig saw. The inside edge of large notch should be 30 to 40 degrees from a centerline drawn perpendicular from flat edge and centered. Notch should be about 2 inches from outside edge to farthest point at center and back of circle.
5. Drill two 1/4-inch holes 5/8 inch from end and 1/4 inch on each side of centerline with a hand drill.
6. Lay this top section on bottom section, keeping flat edges lined up. Locate positions of holes in bottom section and drill two holes as above.
7. Cut top section along centerline to make two identical pieces.
8. Cut 1/4-inch dowel into two pieces 6 1/2 inches long.

9. Cut out back strip 1 × 7 1/2 inches.

10. Drill 1/4-inch hole in end of strip, 1/2 inch down and 1/2 inch in from each side.

11. Finish sanding all edges and check all fits before gluing.

12. Glue together as shown and finish as desired.

When you complete this project, you will have acquired practical experience with a variety of woodworking tools and machinery.

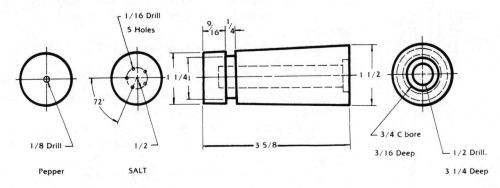

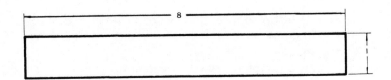

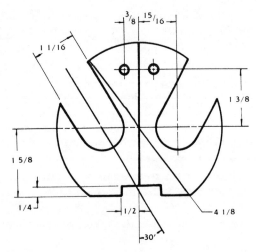
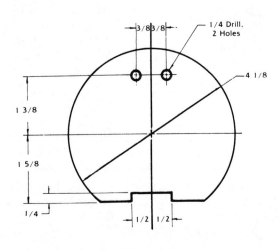

Construction details for spice rack.

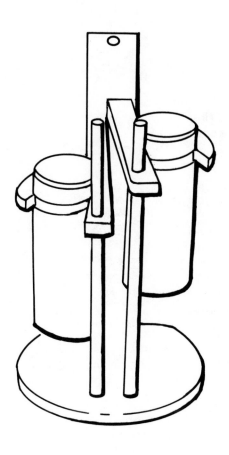

Finished spice rack.

The various components of the set are easy to assemble.

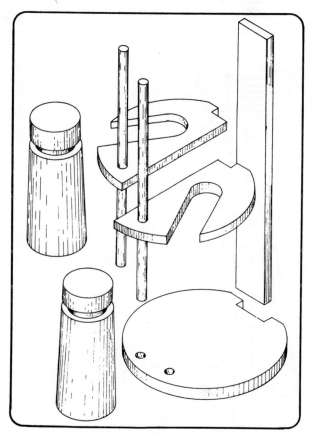

4: Plant Stand
from Scrap Material

Here is a project that will be much in demand by your plant-loving friends. It isn't difficult to make, and you can use left-over wood.

* * *

Using scraps of ripping material and blocks of 1-inch stock, you can build this attractive plant stand.

Oak, mahogany, redwood, fir, and pine give equally good results, especially when finished with a simple clear lacquer and/or oils. Use No. 10 1/4-inch woodscrews for the center fasteners and No. 10 1-inch screws for the top and bottom, along with finishing washers for rigidity.

The project is versatile in terms of both height and diameter size: simply increase the size by proportions approximately equal to the dimensions shown in the diagram. You'll find that after the first few stands are finished, its popularity grows by leaps and bounds!

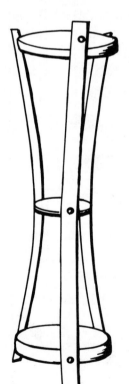

This plant stand is built from scrap material and 1-inch stock.

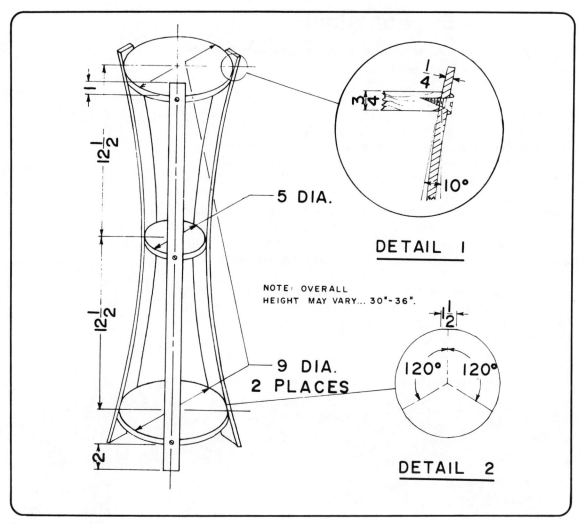

$12\frac{1}{2}$

$12\frac{1}{2}$

2

5 DIA.

9 DIA.
2 PLACES

$\frac{1}{4}$

$\frac{3}{4}$

10°

DETAIL 1

NOTE: OVERALL
HEIGHT MAY VARY... 30"-36".

$\frac{1}{2}$

120°   120°

DETAIL 2

Construction details for plant stand.

5: Footstool

This project allows a lot of room for new woodworkers to practice variation on a basic design.

* * *

Individualization is the key to this footstool project. It is a learning project you will be proud to display. Try designing your own project within certain design and size parameters (maximum dimensions are 10 × 10 × 18 inches).

The project allows you to learn basic operation and safety procedures of: ruler, try square, hand plane, saber saw, band saw, bit brace, router, radial saw, hand sanders, drill press, plug cutter, and screwmate counterbore. You also learn the finishing techniques of stains, staining, lacquers, varnish, and basic polishing.

Choice of wood is left to you. Standard measurements for the stools here are 3/4 × 10 × 17 inches for the top, 3/4 × 10 × 9 1/4 inches for each of the two legs, and 3/4 × 3 × 12 5/8 inches for the brace.

Footstool design.

Alternative footstool design.

PROCEDURE

1. Sketch several designs. Select one, and transfer sketch to three-view drawing, showing all dimensions and details.
2. Complete a bill of materials.
3. Complete a procedure or project construction plan.
4. Secure wood and lay out pattern.
5. Cut out pattern using whatever the saw you've selected.
6. Cut 12-degree angles on legs (both sides) and brace.
7. File and plane where needed. Work legs together so that both are identical.
8. Rout all necessary surfaces using the bit you've selected.
9. Drill holes in legs and brace using screwmate counterbore or equivalent (1 1/2 x 8 screws are suggested).
10. Thoroughly sand all non-joined parts.
11. Assemble with screws and liquid resin glue.
12. Make plugs to fit counterbored holes and fit.
13. Sand plugs level and final sand entire project.

FINISHING

1. Stain desired color.
2. Apply coat of lacquer or varnish; let dry.
3. Sand lightly with 280 grit or finer sandpaper.
4. Apply second coat of finish; let dry.
5. Fine sand.
6. Apply optional third coat of finish; let dry.
7. Fine sand.
8. Apply paste wax, rubbing out with 000 steel wool.
9. Polish with paste wax and soft cloth.

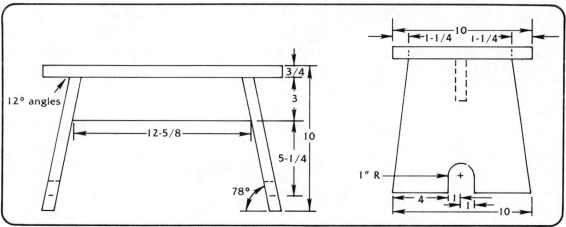

Footstool dimensions.

6: Helmet Bank

Are there young, aspiring woodworkers in the family? Try this project, a football helmet version of the ageless "piggy bank" to spark their interest.

* * *

The project develops many hand skill-oriented functions. The woodworker learns proper uses of the crosscut panel saw, glue and clamps, coping saw, files, drill press, abrasive papers, screws and screwdrivers, acrylic molding oven, buffer, and neatness and patience in painting. The parent or teacher, however, should use the tablesaw and bandsaw.

Before beginning, make a helmet-shaped pattern and a face guard forming jig.

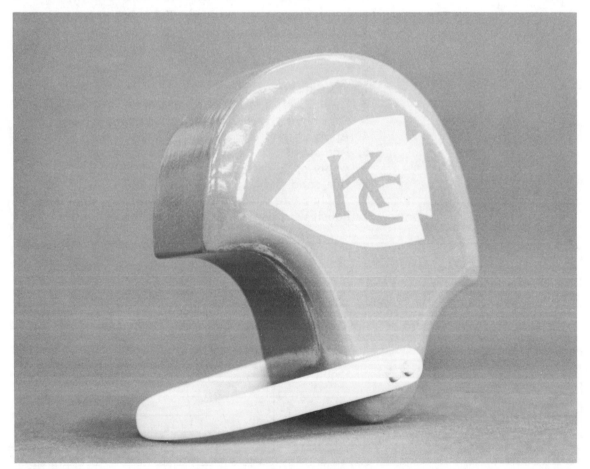

Finished helmet bank.

MATERIALS

Materials include a pine board 3/4 x 5 1/2 x 18 inches; two strips of acrylic 1/4 x 1/2 x 10 inches; polyvinyl glue; methylene or ethylene dichloride; abrasive paper No. 50, No. 100, and No. 150 grit; four 5/8-inch No. 6 round head wood-screws; various colors of enamel paint, and vinyl contact paper.

PROCEDURE

1. Cut an 18-inch section from a 5 1/2-inch wide pine board.
2. Cut this section into three 6-inch pieces.
3. Glue and clamp two pieces face to face.
4. The parent/teacher can resaw the remaining piece on the tablesaw for the outside helmet sections.
5. Trace the pattern shape on the planed faces of the resawed boards. Be sure to reverse the pattern in tracing from one half to the other.
6. Rough shape with a coping saw.
7. Trace the correct pattern on the glued pieces.
8. Rough shape this piece with the coping saw. Cut out the money slot and center section cavity on the bandsaw.
9. Glue and clamp one outside half to the center section (planed faces together).
10. After the glue has set up, remove the clamps and tack the other half in place using finishing nails. Do not drive these nails all the way; they will be removed later. Fill the holes with plastic wood and sand before painting.
11. File the helmet to its finished shape; round the edges.
12. Sand with all three grades of paper.
13. Paint the helmet the color of a favorite team, adding the insignia cut out from contact paper. Don't forget to reverse the pattern.
14. On the table saw, cut out two pieces 1/4 x 1/2 x 10-inch of solid white acrylic. You can pick up scrap pieces. (Note: If plastic is not available, a face guard can be made from wood.)
15. Laminate the plastic together, using either methylene or ethylene dichloride, to form one piece 1/2 x 1/2 x 10 inches.
16. File a 1/4-inch radius on each end corner.
17. Drill two shank holes for screws in each end, with first hole 3/8 inch from end and second hole 5/8 inch from end.
18. File the length to round off the square edge.
19. Sand, pumice, and polish entire piece.
20. Carefully heat the plastic in a shaping oven to 350 degrees Fahrenheit. When flexible, form it around the jig.

21. Once it cools, fit it to the helmet and fasten in place with the roundhead woodscrews. It's complete!

To open the bank, simply remove one screw from the un-glued side and twist. Removing the face mask is not necessary.

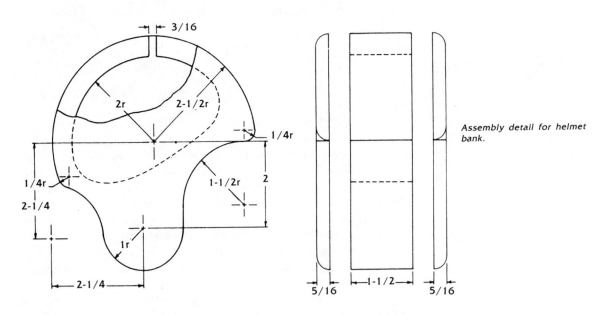

Assembly detail for helmet bank.

Parts for helmet bank.

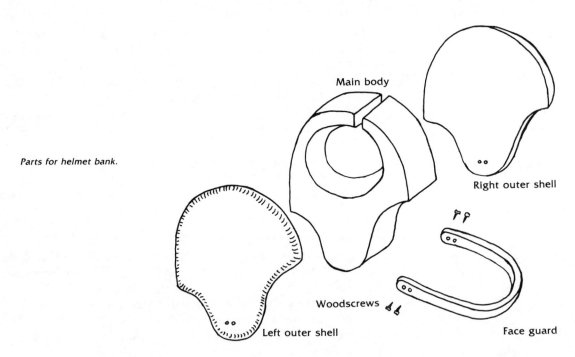

7: Child's Playhouse

Most children love playhouses like the ones pictured here. It would be a larger project, but not a difficult one.

* * *

The log cabin is built of 2-×-4s cut in lengths of 2, 4, and 6 feet with short stop logs of 8 inches. In the rectangular model there is one door and one window, although more window openings can be planned. Nails are used only to assemble the roof rafters, which are held together by a hardboard gusset. The roof is corrugated cardboard held in place by short dowels attached to each side of the outside rafters. The cabin can be built as a square, rectangle, hexagon, or octagon.

The hexagonal fort has two floors. The top floor is attached to the first section by dowels for quick assembly-disassembly.

The cabin and fort seem best suited for indoor use but the four-level playhouse is intended as an out-door project. The playhouse is constructed of four 3/4-×-4-×-8-foot exterior plywood vertical panels on 2-×-4 frames. The cantilever and bottom floor sections are also 3/4-×-4-×-8 exterior plywood on 2-×-6 frames for the base floor.

The three upper cantilever floors are supported by a central 4-×-4 vertical column on the inside and at several points on the outside panels. The roof can be either open or closed. All floors are joined by a ladder attached to the center column. Safety rails are 2-×-3s. The playhouse rests on six concrete piers and is

Old fashioned log cabin playhouse.

37

bolted down to prevent lateral movement. Vertical and floor panels are held together with lag screws and bolts and can be moved quickly and easily.

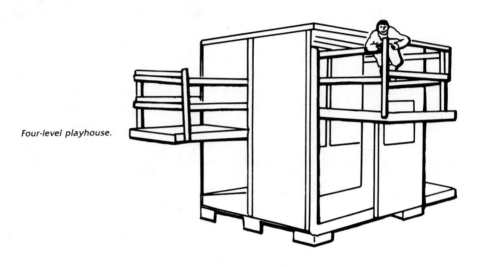

Four-level playhouse.

Two-story fort.

8: Wagon Wheel Magazine Rack

This is an excellent design for a magazine rack. The compartment construction keeps magazines neat and handy.

* * *

The rims of the wheels are laminated. Four pieces of 3/16 × 48-inch stock are glued and shaped around the form which is illustrated elsewhere with this article. The spokes can be fashioned with hand tools or turned on a lathe. The wheelhubs can also be made with hand tools or turned on a lathe.

No. of Pieces	Part	Size
8	Rim	3/16" × 1" × 48"
14	Spokes	3/4" × 1" × 11 1/2"
2	Sides	1" × 1" × 28"
2	Ends	1/2" × 1" × 12"
2	Hubs	2" × 7" × 7"
4	Dividers	3/8" × 9" × 12"
1	Brass Rod	3/8" × 13"
2	Tire (metal)	1/8" × 3/4" × 48"
1	Extruded Metal (bottom)	11" × 11 1/2"

Materials list for magazine rack.

The completed magazine rack.

CONSTRUCTION

Glue and screw the hubs to the stretchers. Glue and screw the rims to the stretcher ends. Locate the centers on the inside edge

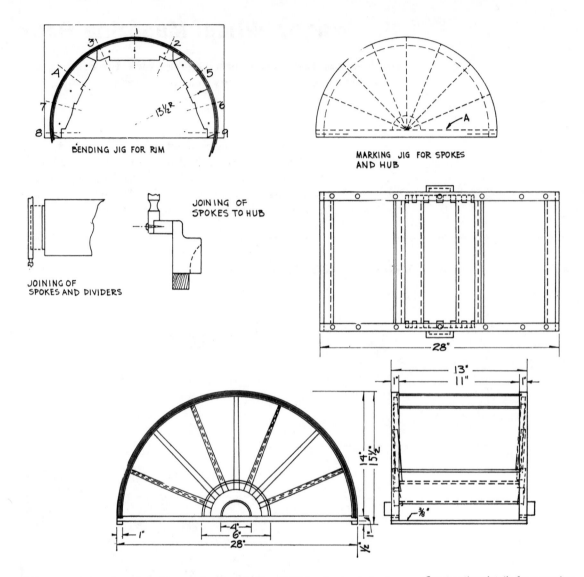

BENDING JIG FOR RIM

MARKING JIG FOR SPOKES AND HUB

JOINING OF SPOKES TO HUB

JOINING OF SPOKES AND DIVIDERS

of the semicircular rim. On each rim, drill a 3/8-inch deep hole. Glue and screw the spokes to the hub and to the rim. Glue and screw wheel units to the cross pieces. Glue and clamp the dividers to the spokes. Insert the brass handle; drill through the rim and pin in place. Screw metal tires to the rims. Attach formed metal bottom to dividers with 3/4-inch, No. 10 blue round head screws.

When bending stock with the rim bending jig, two pieces of rim stock can be glued and formed in one operation with a minimum of breakage. The stock does not have to be steamed or soaked. Clamp application should follow the number order for best results.

Construction details for magazine rack.

9: Spiral Lamp

You will find this hand-carved lamp easy to construct, and many hand and machine processes are used. The carving is not difficult either, and adds intrigue and great beauty to the piece.

* * *

The upright may be made from two pieces of wood glued together. The hole for the lamp cord is made by cutting a 3/16- x -3/8-inch groove in the center of the pieces before they are glued together. If a solid piece of wood is used, the hole is drilled with a 3/8-inch electrician's drill. Each hole is plugged with a scrap piece. When turning is complete, these plugs are drilled out. Recommended wood for this lamp is walnut or mahogany. A hand-rubbed lacquer finish is desirable.

Double spiral carved lamp, and materials list.

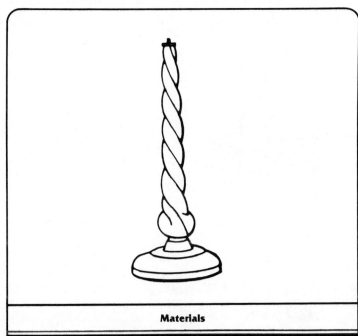

Materials

Part No.	Qty.	Description
1	1	Upright, 2 x 2 x 15
2	1	Upright support 3 x 3 x 5
3	1	Base, 8 x 8 x 4
4	1	Brass nipple, 1/8 x 2
5	1	Lamp harp
6	1	Cord and socket

TURNING

The upright is turned to a plain tapered cylinder divided into 12 equal parts. Circles are made around the cylinder at the divisions by holding a pencil on the "T" rest against each point and revolving the turning by hand. Divide the cylinder lengthwise into four equal parts. Begin at one of the lengthwise divisions and draw a line to the point where the next line and circle intersect. Continue this procedure to the end of the cylinder.

A: 1-3/32"
B: 1 " hole bored 1"

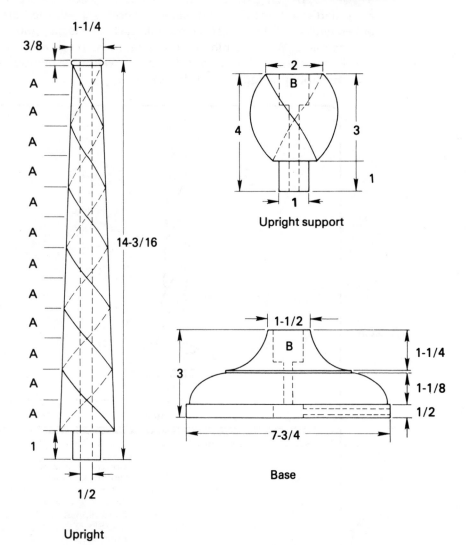

Upright support

Base

Upright

Construction details for spiral lamp.

SECOND SPIRAL

The second spiral line starts on the opposite side of the turning and is laid out in the same manner. With the piece mounted in the lathe, use a backsaw or a crosscut saw to make a 3/8-inch deep cut along one of the spirals. Begin the cut at the large end of the upright and continue to about 1/2-inch from the top. The second cut, made like the first, starts at the opposite side of the turning.

Carving and shaping the spiral are done on the lathe, or a jig may be made to support the upright while carving. The saw kerf is widened and tapered using chisel, wood file, and sandpaper. The spiral is shaped larger at the base and becomes smaller at the top. The upright support is turned to approximate size, removed from the lathe, and the 1-inch hole for the upright is drilled. Remount the assembled pieces; turn to exact size. Lay out and shape spiral on upright support. Turn base to size, drill required holes, assemble, and glue.

10: Mobile Storage
Panel for Lathe Tools

As you become a more experienced woodworker, you will accumulate more tools. This handy storage unit will keep them readily available and easily found—and you can make it yourself.

* * *

This mobile lathe tool storage panel provides about 25 square feet of storage surface, but uses less than 3 square feet of floor space. Mounted on casters, it decentralizes tool storage and provides flexibility for shop management. The panel was initially designed to hold wood lathe tools but can be modified for use with the metal lathe. Silhouettes and color coding permit quick, easy accounting for lathe tools.

Finished mobile storage panel.

44

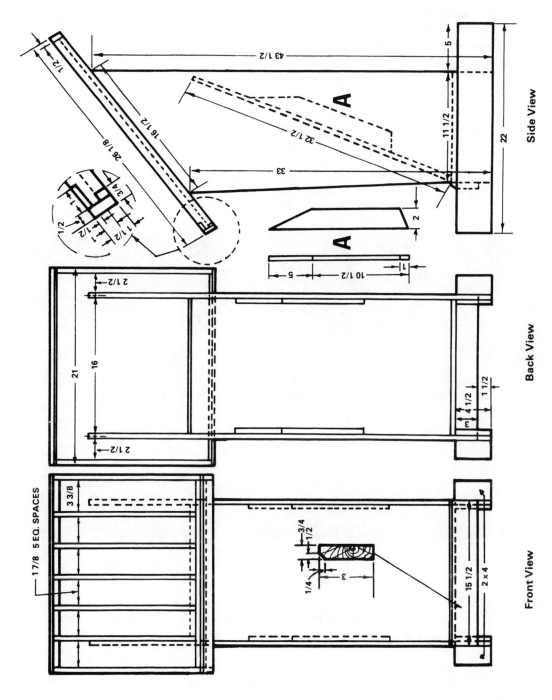

Side View

Back View

Front View

Construction details for mobile storage panel.

45

11: Tool Storage Cart

Here's another unique storage unit. Like the previous project, it is mobile—ideal for shop use—and will keep your tools in their place. They can be color-coded for easy identification, and are inexpensive to make.

* * *

Tools deserve a customized storage system. To achieve easy tool mobility, both within and outside the shop, and maintain a high degree of security and orderliness, use portable carts. The carts are easily rolled into a storage room at the end of the day.

Carts and tools are color coded to identify their home cart. Tools that "disappear" easily can be relocated quickly.

Rolling tool carts have specific places for individual tools.

CONSTRUCTION

Cart construction is simple and surprisingly inexpensive. The carts are made of 1/2-inch plywood. All corners are backed up by 2-x-2-inch or 2-x-4-inch framing members with an 81 degree bevel cut along their edges.

Each tool holder is custom made in multiples of four, so some jigging up will be a wise move. The slanted sides will help keep tools from falling off as the carts are moved. Wood screws, with

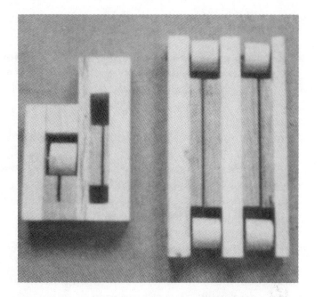

Oak inserts with softwood rollers protect the saw slots from damage.

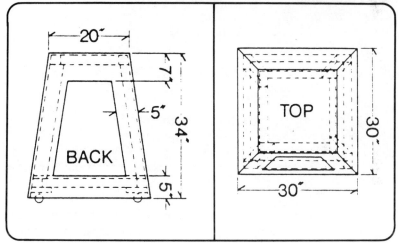

Cart dimensions.

heads cut off and ground smooth, make good strong hangers. Scrap wood blocks should be glued to the inside of the plywood for increased strength where the screws are placed.

The saw slots are protected from cuts by oak inserts under the cart top; the saw teeth strike wooden rollers. A limited amount of storage space is accessible through the rear of each cart.

Paint, handles, and wheels add the final touches. These wheels are 1 5/8-inch in diameter, but larger ones would be needed for rough floors.

12: Paper Saver

Tired of having newspapers lying all over the house? This paper saver is easy to make, and a useful, practical project.

* * *

An average family can accumulate about 21 pounds of paper in a 10-day period. Projected on an annual basis, this represents 766 pounds. When these newspapers are recycled, they can save six and a half trees which would otherwise be cut for pulp. The Paper Saver makes newspaper stacking and storage simple, thus making recycling easier.

Designs may vary with the builder's imagination. Wrought iron is an ideal material—other metals should work equally well. Prepared spindles, available in a number of styles at hardware stores, lumber companies, and through mail order houses, can be used to build attractive paper savers.

PROCEDURE

1. Saw 1 inch off each end of 1 3/4- x -15-inch spindle. These 1-inch pieces will form the legs. Saw spindles in half, sand smooth.

2. One end of cut spindle has threaded hole for threaded wood connector. Spindle is joined with decorative finial. Drops of glue provide a permanent join.

3. Center base end of spindle, drill 3/16-inch hole for lag screw. Lag screw (1/4- x -2-inch) assembles leg, base, and spindle.

4. Final assembly of legs, 3/8- x -16- x -21-inch base (size may vary to fit any newspaper), wood connectors, and finials. Trim with molding and paint or stain.

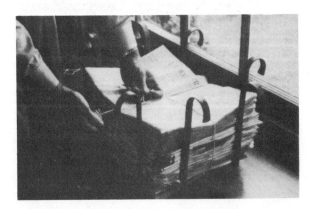

Wrought iron paper saver accents a colonial decor.

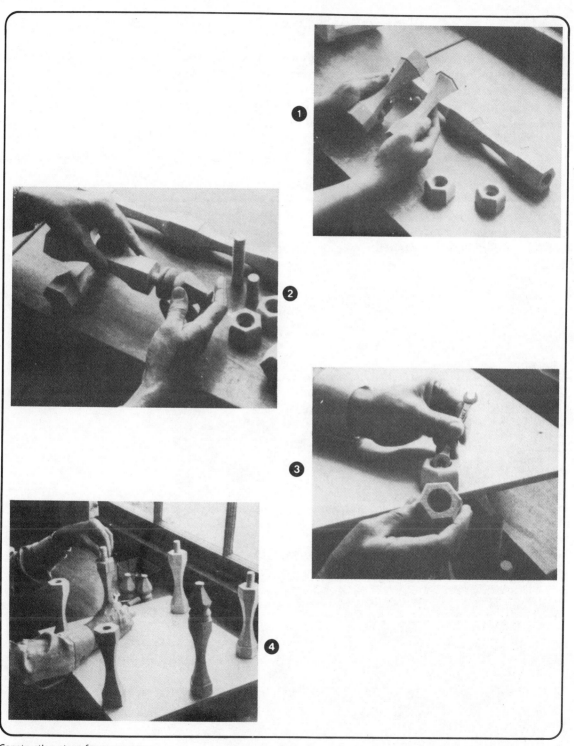

Construction steps for paper saver.

13: Jewelry Box

Before going on to large projects such as chests and cabinets, attempt this smaller project. That way you'll have experience planning and constructing. You can also practice fine woodworking techniques, while keeping the cost down by working in miniature.

* * *

Enlarged, this project would become a chest incorporating the same construction method and joints; thus, the elements of furniture design plus skill development and use of interim procedures and machinery can be taught without having to deal with the soaring materials costs which would accompany a full-size chest project.

Most of the work on this jewelry box can be done on power machinery.

50

| Name of Part of Project | Kind of Material | No. of Pieces | Finish | | | Rough | | | Feet |
			Exact size of Each Piece: Thickness	Width	Length	Rough Size Of Each Piece: Thickness	Width	Length	Bd - Sq - Lin
Sides	Pine	2	1/2	9 1/2"	10"	1/2	10"	12"	1 Bd. Ft.
Top	Pine	1	3/4	10"	14 1/2"	1	12"	15"	1 1/4 Bd. Ft.
Bottom	Pine	1	3/4	10"	14 1/2"	1	12"	15"	1 1/4 Bd. Ft.
Shelves	Pine	4	1/2	9 1/4"	13"	1/2	10"	14"	2 1/2 Bd. Ft.
Drawer front	Pine	1	1/2	8"	12 1/2"	1/2	9"	14"	1 Bd. Ft.
Drawer sides	Pine	1	1/2	2 3/8"	12 3/8"	1/2	3"	10"	1 1/4 Bd. Ft.
Drawer back	Pine	1	1/2	2 3/8"	12 3/8"	1/2	3"	10"	1 1/4 Bd. Ft.
Back	1/8 Hardboard	1	1/8	13"	9 1/4"	1/8	14"	10"	
Drawer bottom	1/8 Hardboard	4	1/8	11 7/8"	9"	1/8	12"	10"	

Note: Plywood is figured by square feet:
Square foot = length × width.

To figure board feet:
No. of Pieces × Thickness × Width × Length

144

Materials list for jewelry box.

CONSTRUCTION

To construct the jewelry box, first use the radial arm saw to cut the rough wood to rough length, and then plane to finish thickness. Use the jointer for joint edging, glue up, and joint the ripped edge; rip if necessary. Cut the material to net length on the circular saw and perform special machine work, sanding, and scraping. Assemble the project and finish sanding.

Apply stain or varnish to the box and perform wet or dry sanding. Apply wax for protection.

You can create variations in the jewelry box by altering the construction method. For example, the simplest (and most expensive) way to build the project is to use solid partitions between drawers. Frame construction between one or more drawers, on the other hand, lowers cost while adding to your experience in construction.

Variations on drawer front styles are usually limited, although others can be developed. The flush drawer front is the simplest but the most exacting in terms of skill requirements because errors in the dadoing are obvious and detract from the appearance of the finished project. One alternative is to hide errors in dados with a finish facing or finishing strips.

The lip drawer will hide various mistakes, but it requires an additional step—an extra rabbet in the construction phase.

Hardware handles are inexpensive and can be purchased at any hardware store or through suppliers' catalogs.

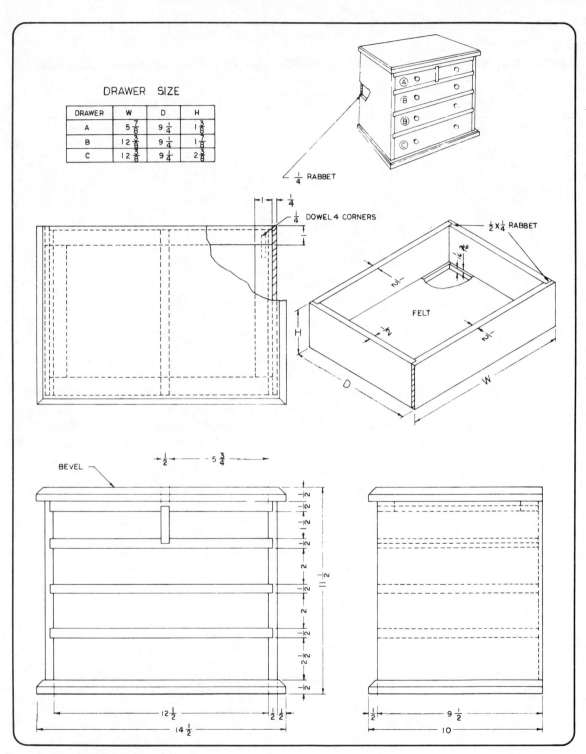

DRAWER SIZE

DRAWER	W	D	H
A	$5\frac{7}{8}$	$9\frac{1}{4}$	$1\frac{3}{8}$
B	$12\frac{3}{8}$	$9\frac{1}{4}$	$1\frac{7}{8}$
C	$12\frac{3}{8}$	$9\frac{1}{4}$	$2\frac{3}{8}$

$\frac{1}{4}$ RABBET

DOWEL 4 CORNERS

$\frac{1}{2}$ X $\frac{1}{4}$ RABBET

FELT

BEVEL

Construction details for jewelry box.

52

14: Platform Rocker

A rocker like this is a welcome addition to any home, and makes a good woodturning project. It is made from hardwood and is comfortable and lightweight.

* * *

This design has 33 turned parts, which are not difficult to make. The important dimensions must be exact and holes drilled in precisely correct positions for all parts to fit as designed. The parts are first turned and roughly sanded. To hold the pieces for turning it is necessary to allow 3/4-inch stubs on the ends that are exposed after assembling. All other pieces are cut to the correct length before turning.

The platform and rockers are neatly sawed from full 1-inch stock. Leave the various surfaces for smoothing later because of danger of scarring while assembling. Because the depth of the rung holes determine the width of the platform and rockers, these should be accurate and square. A bench drill with a large V-block that can be secured to the table is almost a necessity for drilling the holes. A drill vise will hold the rockers square so the leg holes

Materials	
Pioneer Platform Rocker	
2 Back Posts	1 5/8 x 28 3/4
3 Crosspieces	1 x 16 1/4
2 Uprights—panel	1 x 20
1 Panel	1/4 x 10 1/2 x 19 5/8
3 Spindles	1 x 3 1/2
2 Dowels	5/8 x 2 1/2
2 Arms	1 5/8 x 14
2 Arm Posts	1 5/8 x 7 1/2
2 Arm Dowels	3/4 x 3 3/4
2 Braces	1 5/8 x 20 3/4
1 Front Crosspiece	1 5/8 x 21 3/4
1 Back Crosspiece	1 5/8 x 19 1/4
2 Seat Rails	13/16 x 13/16 x 15 1/4
1 Seat Panel	
4 Legs	1 5/8 x 3 1/4
5 Rungs	3/4 x 16 7/8
2 Rockers	1 x 5 x 18
2 Platforms	1 x 5 x 25 1/2
2 Platform Rocker Springs	
1 Foam-Rubber Mat	1 x 15 x 17 1/2
1 Foam-Rubber Mat	1/2 x 10 x 19 1/8
1 Tapestry Cover	12 x 21
1 Tapestry Cover	20 x 24

Materials list and finished platform rocker.

can be drilled. A small level, a T-bevel, and several straight dowels of different sizes will help align the holes.

The front and back crosspieces are next drilled 16 3/8 inch center-to-center for the legs. The back-post holes come in on top of the back-leg holes in the back crosspiece but at an angle of 13 degrees, slanting backward. The holes for the seat rails are drilled 14 inches center-to-center at right angles to the leg holes and 1/4 inch above center. The seat rails are left square but the arrises are heavily sanded after turning the ends. Assemble the bottom parts and wait until the rest is together before putting in the panel. A wood file and a pocket knife can be used to an advantage in bringing the turned joints together.

Drill the arm holes 1 inch deep, 9 inches center-to-center. The drill table is tilted to 66 degrees for drilling the holes in the brace. The brace is fastened to the back post with a 5/8-inch dowel, the hole for it being 1 1/4 inches deep and at right angles to the arm-post holes. The brace goes over the end of the front crosspiece. A 3/4-inch hole, 1 1/4 inches deep will be needed. Due to the spread of the arms in front, this hole will enter at 88 degrees, slanting towards the back.

The back posts are drilled on the inside with a 3/4-inch drill. The 5/8-inch brace hole is drilled 1 1/4 inch deep on the outside and 2 degrees towards the back side because of the spread of the arms. The center and upper crosspieces are drilled with 11/16-inch holes, 11 inches center-to-center for the uprights along the panel. The center and lower crosspieces are drilled with three 5/8-inch holes 4 3/4 inches center-to-center for the spindles.

Assemble the entire chair. The spring holes illustrated are for a popular spring but, if not available, others can be used. Install them with short screws. Check the idle position of the back so that its top is just back of the ends of the platform and the arms slant backward a small amount. The rocker should operate comfortably.

The seat and back panels should be located on all pieces before assembling. These grooves can be cut on the dado saws of the table saw. No real difficulty is experienced but a little ingenuity will have to be used in holding the pieces from rolling. The old rockers often used webbing to support the upholstering. Panels upholstered with foam rubber are much neater and lighter. The back panel is made to fit loosely in its groove so that the tapestry can be tacked along its edge before inserting permanently in the groove.

The platform and rockers have flutes routed on the outside to add to the design. Then surface all faces before sanding. Next fine sand all other parts. Remove the stubs and smooth off the

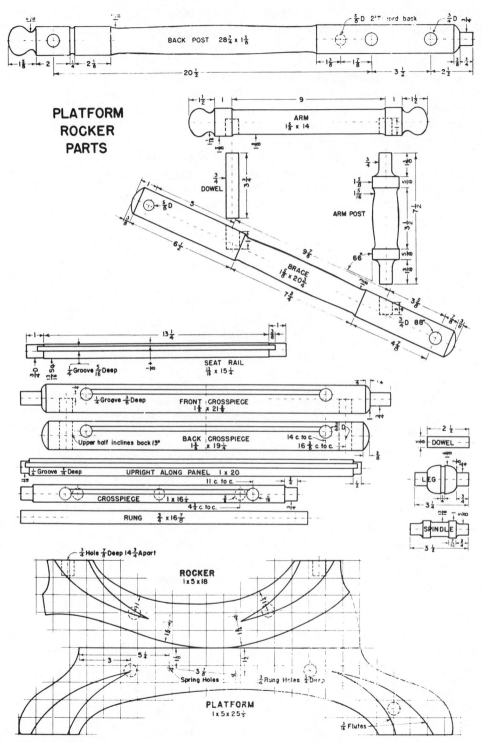

PLATFORM ROCKER PARTS

Construction details for platform rocker.

ends. (A chuck can be made to hold the parts which cannot be held between lathe centers so that they can be slowly turned for finishing.

After finishing all parts, upholster the back using 1/2-inch foam rubber under the tapestry. The seat panel, rails, and crosspieces are assembled with glue. They are upholstered with 1-inch foam rubber under the tapestry which is brought around the rails and crosspieces and tacked on the under side.

Glue the other parts together in logical order, protecting the surfaces where clamps are needed. Finally, install the springs again and, if they operate satisfactorily, fasten them with large screws. By making this platform rocker, you can obtain many experiences on woodworking machines other than the lathe.

15: Folding Fisherman's Chair

Any fisherman or sportsman will appreciate this item. It is portable, easy to carry anywhere—and it has a storage unit.

* * *

You can enjoy a variety of construction processes here, and the total cost is reasonable. The instructions and parts list follow.

Part	Size	Comment
1. back	15 1/2 × 3 1/2 × 1/2	Secure the back with screws
2. arms (2)	12 × 3 1/2 × 1/2	Curve the arms and sand them for comfort. The arms also act as locks for the drawers to assemble them square.
3. pivot ass'y (2)	1/4 × 2 1/2" lag screw & washer	Bore the holes carefully at 1 1/8" from the surface of the seat. Allow for the handle. Note: If the seat is to be upholstered you must allow for the padding.
4. handle	3/4 dowel	Secure the handle with No. 10 or 12 screws.
5. seat	13 1/2 × 12 × 1/2	More than 1/4" stock is necessary to keep the seat rigid.
6. drawer	1/4 & 1/8	Build this drawer large for those bulky items such as finishing reels and food.
7. door	1/8 stock	Hinge the door to the seat edge and install a catch. This compartment is for storage of the legs.
8. end blocks (2)	1 1/2 × 3 1/2 × 2	Be careful when nailing in these blocks because 3/4" holes for the legs must be bored into them.
9. side	13 1/2 × 3 1/2 × 1/2	Cut a groove into the sides for a drawer glide and dado for the center brace.
10. center brace	3 1/2 × 1/2	This is an optional unit if a larger drawer or open space is desired; however, a heavy seat is then needed to support the weight without a sag.
11. bottom	13 1/2 × 12 1/2 × 1/4	You may wish to cover this surface with a non-scratching material if the seat will be used in a boat without the legs installed.
12. front	13 1/2 × 3 1/2 × 1 1/2	Cut a groove(s) and dado to match the ones in the side piece. Bore holes for the pole holders.
13. drawers (2)	1/4 to 1/16 stock	Build these small drawers to fit your needs. Use waterproof glues.
14. legs (4)	10 1/2 × 3/4 tube	Bore the holes at an angle and to the proper size for a snug fit. Secure with set screws or pins.

Materials list and procedure for fisherman's chair.

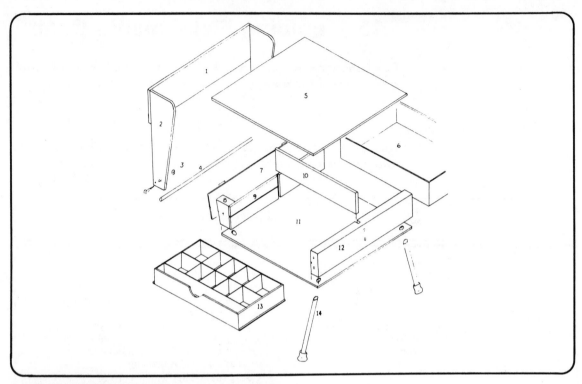

Take off the legs and fold down the seat back and you have a chair that can be carried to any sporting event.

There are drawers for fishing equipment and holes to hold the poles. A padded seat is a comfort option.

58

16: Wall Clock

Simple lines, fine wood, and a battery-powered movement combine to make a pleasing and challenging project. There's another plus included: learn how to etch the glass case and give the piece a personal, quality touch.

* * *

Building this wall clock will give you an opportunity to explore a variety of construction experiences and develop problem-solving skills.

The clock is constructed around a battery-powered movement available through many arts and crafts mail-order firms. These movements are surprisingly accurate and reasonable in price.

The project makes extensive use of the table saw or the radial arm saw for most operations, including the production of the top and door molding stock. For a finishing touch to the clock, etch the glass door.

MATERIALS

Use walnut, mahogany, or pine for the clock case. Mount the face and movement on a piece of fiberboard covered with several coats of flat black enamel. The door is single strength window glass.

Carefully select lumber for grain and figure, then dress to the appropriate thicknesses. Cut the back from one piece of solid stock, or glue-up to suit. The back has a 3/16-x-3/16-inch tongue on either edge to match corresponding grooves on the case sides. Cut case sides to size, with grooves to match the back. Cut the top and bottom; chamfer the bottom 45 degrees × 1/4 inch on three sides. Rabbet the top on all sides to fit inside the case and give the appearance of being only 1/4 inch thick, while at the same time providing a means of attachment.

Assemble the rail for the top, using a mortise and tenon joint for attaching to the case sides. Cut a 1/8-inch groove along the bottom to receive the panel and movement. Cut the bottom rail with matching tenons for corresponding mortise in the case sides.

To produce the molding stock, make two angular cuts and round-over the edges with a small hand plane. Commercial molding may also be used.

Finished wall clock.

Materials		
Qty.	*Description*	
2	Sides, 5/8″ × 3-5/8″ × 20-3/4″	
1	Back, 3/8″ × 8-1/4″ × 20-3/4″	
1	Top, 5/8″ × 4-1/2″ × 11″	
1	Bottom, 5/8″ × 4″ × 10″	
1	Bottom rail, 5/8″ × 3/4″ × 8-1/4″	
1	Top rail (two pieces glued together), 5/8″ × 2-5/8″ × 8-1/4″	
1	Backing on top rail, 5/8″ × 5/8″ × 8-1/4″	
1	Top molding, 3/4″ × 1-1/8″ × 20″	
1	Door frame, 5/8″ × 3/4″ × 56″	
1	Brass latch with screws	
2	Brass butt hinges and screws, 1″ × 1″	
1	Brass hanger with screws	
4	Dowels, 1/4″ dia × 3/4″	
1	Single strength glass, 7-1/2″ × 16″	
4	Glazer points	
2	Round head brass screws, No. 4 × 5/8″	
1	Tempered fiberboard panel, 1/8″ × 7-7/8″ × 8-1/16″	
1	Battery movement and satin brass dial (available from Lee Wards, 1200 St. Charles Rd., Elgin, IL 60120)	

Materials list for wall clock.

PROCEDURE

1. Finish sand all parts.

2. Apply glue to the joints of the back, sides, and upper and lower front rails.

3. Carefully fit the pieces together and clamp with moderate pressure. Remove excess glue from the joints and check for squareness.

4. Position, glue, and clamp the two fiberboard panel attachment blocks to both sides of the case.

5. Prepare dowel joints for the bottom and case.

6. Glue and clamp the top and bottom to the case. (If steps 3 and 6 are completed after applying finish, first cover the glue surfaces with masking tape.)

7. Make the miter cuts for the top molding. Use small wedges to facilitate clamping. Apply glue and clamp.

8. Make miter cuts for the door molding (a reinforced joint is suggested) and glue using miter clamps.

9. Using 220 garnet paper, lightly sand all exposed areas.

10. Apply appropriate filler-stain according to product directions.

11. Apply clear finish to suit; rub with 4/0 steel wool.

12. Fit hinges to door frame and case.

13. Mount movement and dial to fiberboard panel and install in case.

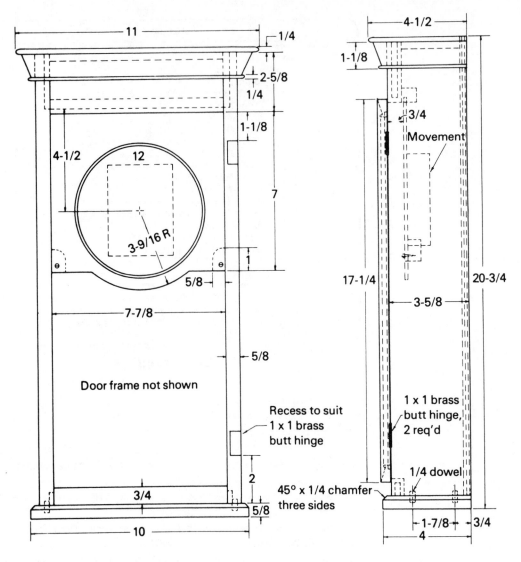

Construction details for wall clock.

14. Install glass in door using small glazer joints. If hardwood is used, a small hole drilled where the glazer point is to be located will reduce installation effort.

15. Install remaining hardware and attach pendulum to movement.

16. Adjust pendulum length for most accurate timekeeping.

ETCHING GLASS

Etching a design on glass can be done by sandblasting, which is a contemporary industrial process used for all kinds of cleaning, surface preparation, and texturization. The theory of the process is simple: (1) A granular abrasive is moved by air pressure to (2) abrade a hard surface, and (3) a resilient material prevents the abrasive from etching the undesired areas. Basically, the abrasive strikes the unprotected glass, making very fine chips in the surface while bouncing off the resilient masking tape.

Consider these points when sandblasting. Air pressure should be 60 to 80 psi; exceeding this may cause the abrasive to penetrate the masked areas. Hold the blasting nozzle perpendicular to the work, being careful not to get too close to the work surface. The abrasive grain size will determine the "texture" or "softness" of the etched surface. The finer the abrasive, the softer the texture. Etch only long enough to obtain a good texture; etching too long reduces the clarity of fine detail and eventually erodes the masking tape. The finished design will be as faithfully reproduced as you have cut it.

Procedure

1. Sketch or trace a full-sized line drawing of the material to be etched on the glass.

2. Carefully mask-off the entire glass surface with two layers of masking tape set at right angles to each other and lapping over to the opposite side. Normally, etching is done on the reverse side of a pane; the line drawing must be in *reverse* so that when facing the completed work it will read correctly.

3. Apply the line drawing to the masked surface with rubber cement. Be careful in aligning and centering the design. Frequently "measured centering" appears optically unbalanced or offcenter.

4. Using a frisket knife or sharp stencil knife, cut through the masking tape along the lines of the design, carefully overlapping intersecting lines. Make sure that straight cuts are "true" and curved lines are "fair." If you accidentally strip-out or make a bad cut, just remask that portion.

5. After cutting and striping, inspect the work carefully, because sandblasting will etch very fine detail. Make necessary corrections.

6. Follow normal safety precautions when using sandblasting equipment. Using an air pressure of 60 to 80 psi and fine or medium grade silica or aluminum oxide abrasive, proceed to the etching (blasting) process. Be sure to hold the blasting nozzle perpendicular to the work. Blast the exposed surface sufficiently to uniformly frost the surface and bring out detail.

7. After blasting, hold glass to the light and inspect;

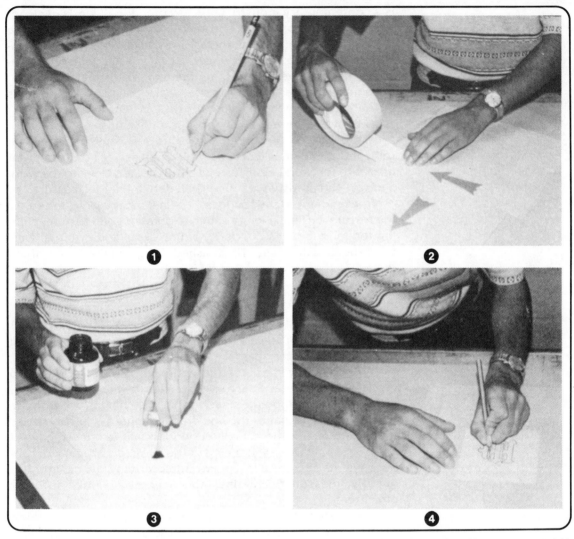

Steps to etching. 1) Sketch a full-size pattern on paper. 2) Tape entire glass area with two layers of masking tape, set at right angles and overlapped. 3) Center and align the line drawing on the taped glass and secure it with rubber cement. 4) Cut through the masking tape, overlapping intersecting lines.

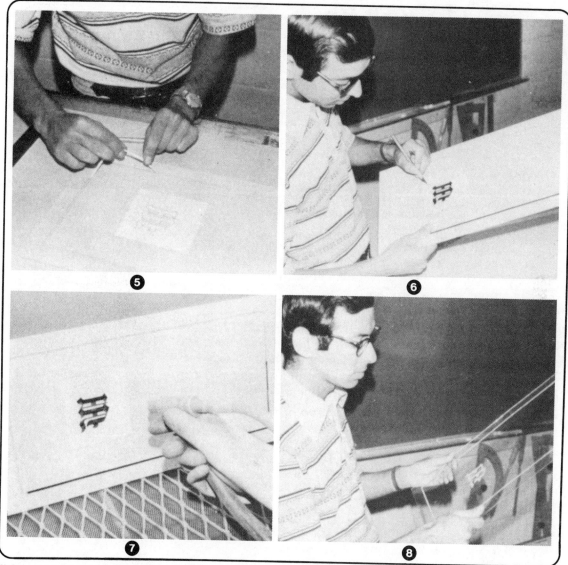

5) Strip out the border on the edge of the glass window and make necessary corrections. 6) Inspect design, making sure that details are accurate. Remask bad areas and recut. 7) Uniformly sandblast the design, keeping the nozzle at right angles to the work. 8) Inspect the finished product, reblast where necessary. Remove tape and clean glass.

correct any areas not etched or frosted by another run through the process.

8. Remove masking tape from glass and clean carefully.

This technique can be used on an unlimited variety of materials, including plastics, ceramics, metals, particleboard, fiberboard, etc. Sandblasting wood will achieve a weathered or driftwood appearance.

17: Wall Mirror

Wall mirrors date back to the colonial era, where they were used near entrances of homes. You can make your own for about one-quarter the price you would expect to pay retail. Design variations include a planter, coat hanger, and clock.

* * *

PROCEDURE

1. Lay out patterns on 3/4-inch wood (we used pine).
2. Rough cut all parts, starting with side lengths. A 1-x-12-inch board will cut into two sides, top, and valances.
3. Lay out patterns for valances, sides, and support.
4. Cut 30-degree angles on side and top pieces.
5. On a band, jig, or sabre saw, cut out pieces to shape.
6. Cut out shelf to size and notch edges to accept sides as shown.
7. Sand all parts (except edges to be joined) with 150 grit sandpaper.
8. Attach the top valance, back support, and bottom valance to one side using glue and 1 1/2-inch finishing nails or brads. Placement of bottom valance is optional. Note: For proper fit, the top valance, bottom valance, back support, and shelf (notch to notch) must all be the same width.
9. Place shelf support and shelf in position; nail.
10. Rout a 1/4-inch rabbet joint into the back for the mirror; leave enough room to fasten with glazing points. If no router is available, the mirror can be attached with nails or metal corner brackets.
11. Cut a 1/2-inch hole in the center of the back support for a hanging point.
12. Attach top flush with the back.
13. Final sand with 150 grit and 220 grit paper. For an extra smooth finish, rub down with 000 steel wool.

FINISHING

1. Remove dust particles from all pieces.
2. Apply stain according to manufacturer's directions.
3. Apply either varnish or lacquer in a very light coat. Dilute two parts sealer to 1/2 part solvent. Although varnish is more difficult to apply, it is the more durable finish.
4. After first coat dries, lightly sand with very fine sand-

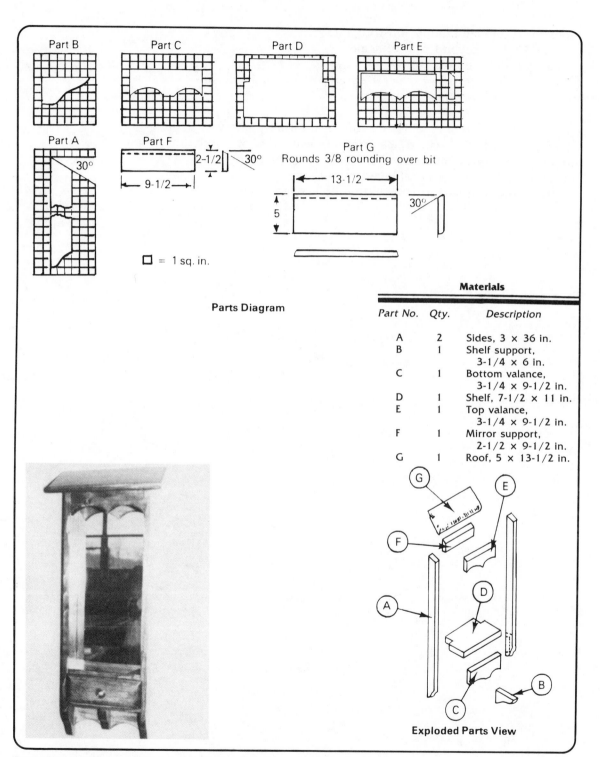

Part B

Part C

Part D

Part E

Part A

30°

Part F

2-1/2 | 30°

9-1/2

Part G
Rounds 3/8 rounding over bit

13-1/2

5

30°

□ = 1 sq. in.

Parts Diagram

Materials

Part No.	Qty.	Description
A	2	Sides, 3 × 36 in.
B	1	Shelf support, 3-1/4 × 6 in.
C	1	Bottom valance, 3-1/4 × 9-1/2 in.
D	1	Shelf, 7-1/2 × 11 in.
E	1	Top valance, 3-1/4 × 9-1/2 in.
F	1	Mirror support, 2-1/2 × 9-1/2 in.
G	1	Roof, 5 × 13-1/2 in.

Exploded Parts View

Construction details, materials list, and finished wall mirror.

paper to remove all bumps and roughness.

    5. Apply a second coat of sealer.

    6. Repeat step 4.

    7. Apply final coat of sealer. If spray sealer is available, apply this coat by spraying.

    8. Repeat step 4.

    9. Dip 000 steel wool into a can of furniture paste wax; rub entire project. Buff with a clean cloth; repeat. After repeated rubbings, apply wax with a dampened clean cloth; continue to buff until desired luster is achieved.

    10. Install the mirror with glazing points, and hang.

18: Sign Making

Sign making is a hobby you could turn into a part-time business. Given the basics, there is much room to develop your own ideas. Use your creativity!

* * *

In this project you use various woodworking equipment: band-saw, radial arm saw, drill press, router. You can also experiment with mortise and tenon joints, and design your own components, such as the spindles and decorative aprons. The inscription and relief carving are also left to your imagination.

CONSTRUCTION

Body. The body of the sign is fabricated from two pieces of pine approximately 1 1/4 x 7 x 18 inches. Cut tenons on each end, using the radial arm saw for the shoulder cuts. Transfer the inscription and carving design to the wood with carbon paper. Use a router with a 1/4-inch straight bit to incise the lettering freehand. Fit the drill press with a Forstner bit to relieve the area around the carving. Use chisels, gouges, and rifflers to complete the carving.

Rails. Cut the rails 3/4 x 2 x 17 inches from pine. After laying out the mortises, use the drill press and Forstner bit combination to remove most of the wood, and finish the mortises with a chisel. In most cases the tenons need to be trimmed slightly with a rabbet plane to obtain an accurate fit.

Aprons. Decorative aprons are employed at the top and bottom of the sign. Cut the aprons from 3/4-inch pine with the band-saw. Rip 3/4- x -3/4-inch cleats from scrap, and chamfer on all exposed corners. Later these will be screwed and glue to the aprons, and then to the rails.

Legs. Use 2 x 2-inch turning stock for the legs. Cut them 3 inches longer than the body of the sign and, after rough turning, form a 3/4-inch round tenon on each end.

ASSEMBLY

Before assembly, sand all components with No. 100, then No. 180 abrasive paper. Use a brace and bit to bore holes for the round tenons. Glue up the legs, rails, and body simultaneously using white glue and bar clamps. After installing the aprons, scrape off any excess glue, and finish sanding with No. 220 paper.

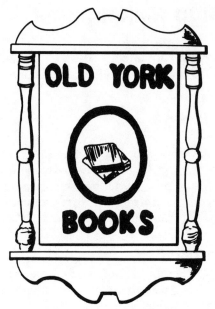

Design your own carvings, aprons, and legs for sign.

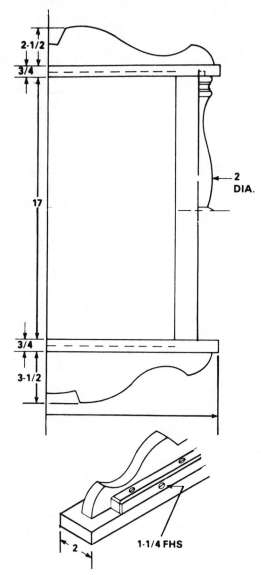

Construction details for sign.

FINISH

First stain the entire project. You might prefer to stain the lettering and carved areas with a contrasting stain. You could also use a propane torch to char highlights on the carving. Apply two to three coats of clear wood finish, and sand lightly with No. 280 paper after each coat. Give the project a final finish with paste wax, using steel wool to rub in the wax and a soft cloth to buff up a high gloss.

19: Stereo Speaker Cabinet

Have you ever considered constructing your own stereo system? It can be done—here is a great place to start.

* * *

We found, by experimenting with enclosures of different designs, that merely building a wooden enclosure and mounting a speaker inside simply did not bring about desirable results. Various models were tried and/or modified, and the following design was found to produce the best sound quality.

This cabinet is planned for use with a single 12-inch full-range speaker—either the two- (coaxial) or three-way (triaxial) type—with a built-in crossover system.

Speaker cabinets.

Speakers of different sizes require different amounts of enclosed air space. Basically, this is a problem of employing or not employing a baffle or reflex port. A cabinet containing 20 to 35 cubic feet of air space would be required if no baffle were used, but would be entirely too large for residential use. Obviously some type of a baffle system must be included to reduce the enclosure to a reasonable size. Eight-inch speakers require a minimum enclosure volume of 2 cubic feet; 12-inch speakers, at least 4-inch cubic feet; and 15-inch speakers, 8 cubic feet or more.

The problem of reflected sound is handled through the design of the reflex port itself, as well as the ample use of insulation (2-inch fiberglass works well). Notice the two different sources of sound—the direct, which leaves the speaker and travels through the reflex port; and the indirect, which reflects against the insulation-lined sides, back, top, and bottom. All sounds finally exit through the elliptical opening in the front panel of the cabinet.

Woodworkers will have different needs as far as the overall physical dimensions of their own speaker cabinets. Some of them may wish to enclose the entire stereo system, components and speakers, in one basic cabinet unit. Obviously there will have to be changes in the dimensions, but even though the overall sizes were often changed in the past, the results were very good as long as the basic concepts of the reflex port, the volume of minimum air space, and the use of fiberglass insulation were maintained.

PROCEDURE

1. Plywood should be used whenever possible because it is not likely to warp or split, and adds rigidity to the final product. We used 3/8-inch interior plywood for the front and back, while the speaker mount was made from 3/4-inch plywood. Veneer plywood, 3/4-inch grade A-C, is recommended for the sides. Solid 3/4-inch thick wood is needed for the top and bottom, due to the exposed edges (see C, Detail B).

2. Use flat-head-steel wood screws, No. 10-x-1 1/2-inch, to install the speaker mount, and 3/4- x -3/4- x -8-inch wood strips for holding the mount in place. (Do not glue.)

3. The wooden baffles (see C, Detail C) can be made from scrap lumber. Laminate pieces of stock to a thickness of 3 1/2 inches. Use the band saw for final shaping. Use No. 10-x-1 1/4-inch flathead wood screws to attach these baffles to the speaker mount. The speakers can be installed with No. 10- x -1-inch round-head wood screws or 3/16-x-1 1/2-inch round-head stove bolts and washers. (This may vary according

72

to the size and make of the speaker.)

4. Before placing the speaker cloth over the front of the cabinet, cover the elliptical opening with several thicknesses of dark cloth material. A standard stapler can be used for attaching both types of cloth. (Be careful to keep the pattern of the material parallel with the edges of the cabinet.)

5. Fiberglass insulation should be used on the inside of the cabinet. The 2-inch-thick building type is adequate, and can be affixed with No. 6 carpet tacks or staples.

6. The legs (see C, Detail A) can be fastened to the cabinet with four 5/16- x -2 1/2-inch hanger bolts, and either straight or angled table-leg brackets. Use round-head-steel wood screws, No. 8- x -5/8 inch, to fasten the brackets to the bottom of the cabinet.

7. Drill one 1/4-inch diameter hole in the back of the cabinet for the entry of the feed line from the amplifier. Number 18-gauge lamp cord can be used for this feed line.

8. To install the front and back plywood panels in the cabinet use No. 4- x -3/4-inch flat-head-steel wood screws. (Do not glue these panels in place.)

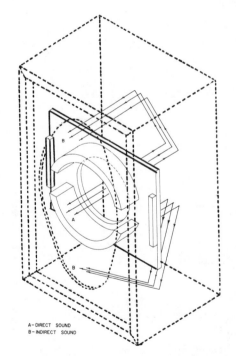

A – DIRECT SOUND
B – INDIRECT SOUND

How sound can be controlled through the use of a reflexport type speaker cabinet.

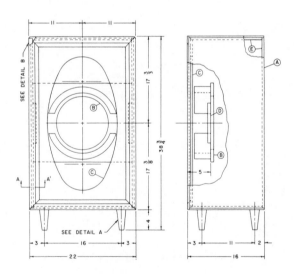

Construction details for speaker cabinets.

LETTER	DESCRIPTION
A	RABBET BOTTOM, TOP & SIDES 3/8 X 3/8 TO RECEIVE PLYWOOD BACK. BACK IS 3/8 PLYWOOD, 21 1/4 X 34.
B	SPEAKER MOUNT & BAFFLE SEE DETAIL C.
C	CABINET FRONT. SEE DETAIL D.
D	WOODEN STRIP, 3/4 X 3/4 X 8.
E	APPLY TWO-INCH FIBERGLASS INSULATION TO ALL MAIN INTERIOR SURFACES OF CABINET.

DETAIL B

SECTION A-A'

45°

$\frac{1}{4}$ R.

$\frac{1}{4}$

$\frac{3}{4}$

2

DETAIL A

1" D.

4

2 D.

IF BRASS FERRULES ARE USED, THE 1" DIAMETER WILL
VARY. FERRULES MUST BE CUSTOM FIT.
LEGS MAY BE PLACED ON 15 DEGREE SLANT BY USING
ANGLED BRACKETS.

DETAIL D

33

8

$8\frac{1}{2}$

$8\frac{1}{2}$

8

$10\frac{1}{8}$

$20\frac{1}{4}$

$10\frac{1}{8}$

22 R

5 R

$\frac{3}{8}$ PLYWOOD

MOUNT SPEAKER

$\frac{3}{4}$ PLYWOOD

$3\frac{1}{2}$

$4\frac{1}{4}$

DETAIL C

16

8

8

$10\frac{1}{4}$

$20\frac{1}{2}$

$10\frac{1}{4}$

2

2

$10\frac{3}{4}$ D.

$7\frac{1}{4}$ R.

6 R

More construction details for speaker cabinets.

74

20: Wooden Chest

This small chest is beautiful for any home. It's especially nice at the foot of a bed, for storing blankets.

* * *

CONSTRUCTION

Most pieces are small enough to use No. 1 common stock without any gluing for width.

Follow the following diagrams for construction.

Various "extras" can be added. For example, the chest could be cedar-lined, a tray could be added, or locking mechanisms or decorative hardware could be installed.

Materials			
Qty.	Part	Assembly	Dimensions
4	End stiles	F&B	3/4 × 2-1/2 × 15-1/4
4	Small panels	F&B	1/2 × 7 × 11-3/4
2	Large panels	F&B	1/2 × 10-1/2 × 11-3/4
4	Rails	F&B	3/4 × 2 × 27-1/2
4	Center stiles	F&B	3/4 × 2 × 11-3/4
4	Rails	End	3/4 × 2 × 11-1/2
4	Panels	End	1/2 × 5 × 11-3/4
4	End stiles	End	3/4 × 2 × 15-1/4
2	Center Stiles	End	3/4 × 2 × 11-3/4
1	Bottom	Bottom	5/8 × 13-3/4 × 30
2	Frame ends	Bottom	3/4 × 2-1/2 × 18
2	Frame sides	Bottom	3/4 × 2-1/2 × 34

Materials list for wooden chest.

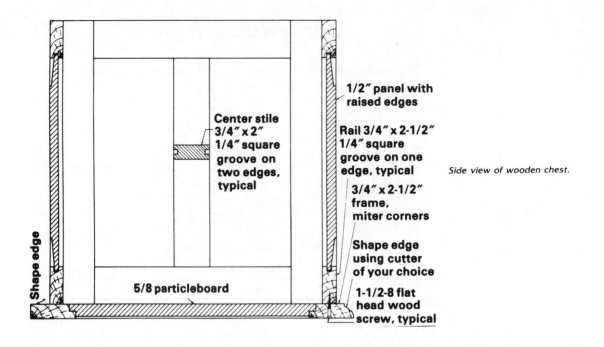

Center stile
3/4" x 2"
1/4" square
groove on
two edges,
typical

1/2" panel with
raised edges

Rail 3/4" x 2-1/2"
1/4" square
groove on one
edge, typical

3/4" x 2-1/2"
frame,
miter corners

Shape edge
using cutter
of your choice

1-1/2-8 flat
head wood
screw, typical

Shape edge

5/8 particleboard

Side view of wooden chest.

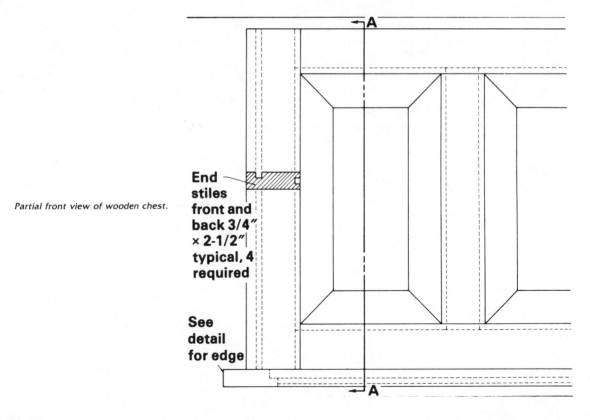

A

End
stiles
front and
back 3/4"
× 2-1/2"
typical, 4
required

See
detail
for edge

A

Partial front view of wooden chest.

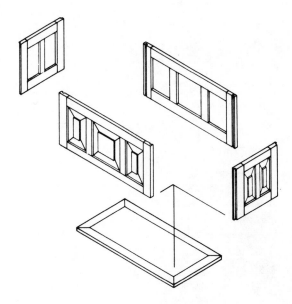

Exploded view of wooden chest.

Corner detail of wooden chest.

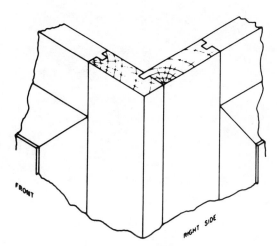

FRONT

RIGHT SIDE

Finished wooden chest. Insert shows another leg design.

21: Guncase/China Cabinet

Are you ready for a large project? This one can be modified for use in various rooms of your home.

* * *

Cabinet-making skills are useful in making many kinds of wood furniture, such as desks, china or kitchen cabinets, chests, etc. The value of constructing this gun or china cabinet lies in the reinforcement of such versatile skills, including cutout, assembly, applying trim, working with hardware and adjustable shelving, drawer construction, and finishing. Follow the drawings for either guncase or china cabinet, but note the upper assembly modification needed to make the china cabinet. Either wood frame or sliding glass doors are well suited to both types of cabinet.

Use poplar frame for the upper and lower parts of the cabinet and 3/4-inch birch plywood, good two sides, for the sides. The shelves can be made of plywood or pine shelving. Connect the upper and lower cabinets with 1/4-inch stove bolts fastened under the felt bottom gunbutt board. Finish with exterior trim, stain, and spray lacquer.

The finished cabinet.

Materials

Part	Qty.	Description
1	2	3/4 × 10 × 30-1/2 pine
2	2	3/4 × 2 × 28 poplar
3	2	3/4 × 2 × 54 poplar
4	2	3/4 × 10-1/4 × 54 birch plywood
5	1	1/4 × 31-1/4 × 54 felt on plywood
6	2	3/4 × 15-1/4 × 22 birch plywood
7	1	3/4 × 15 × 30-1/2 plywood
8	1	3/4 × 2 × 11 poplar
9	1	3/4 × 3 × 28 poplar
10	2	3/4 × 2 × 28 poplar
11	2	3/4 × 2 × 22 poplar
12	1	3/4 × 15-3/4 × 33 birch plywood
13	1	1/4 × 31-1/4 × 22 plywood
trim (12)	1	3/4 × 1 × 70 poplar
doors	2	3/4 × 13-1/2 × 11-1/2 birch plywood
drawer	1	3/4 × 4-1/2 × 28-1/2 birch plywood
hinge	8	3/8 offset brass
pull	2	3" o.c. brass
knob	4	1-1/4 brass
trim	2	2" cap × 36" poplar
bolts	4	3/8 × 2 steel
felt	1	1 yard × 54" felt

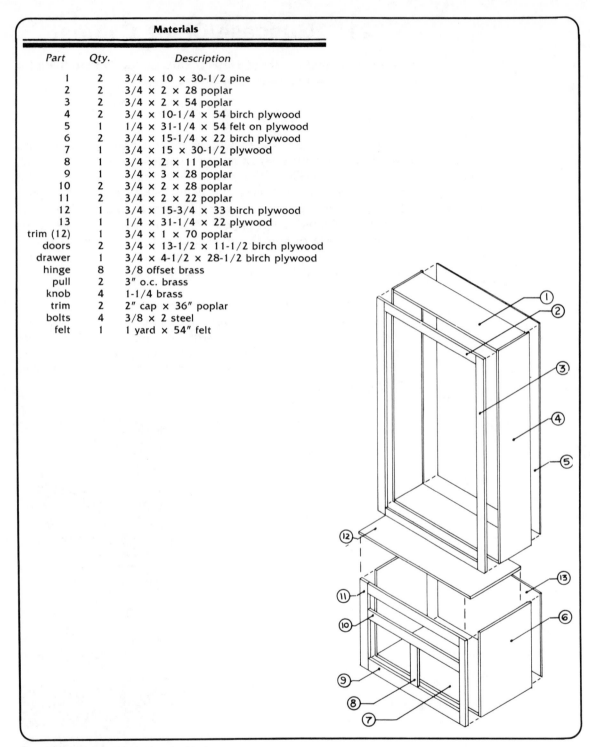

Materials list and exploded view of cabinet.

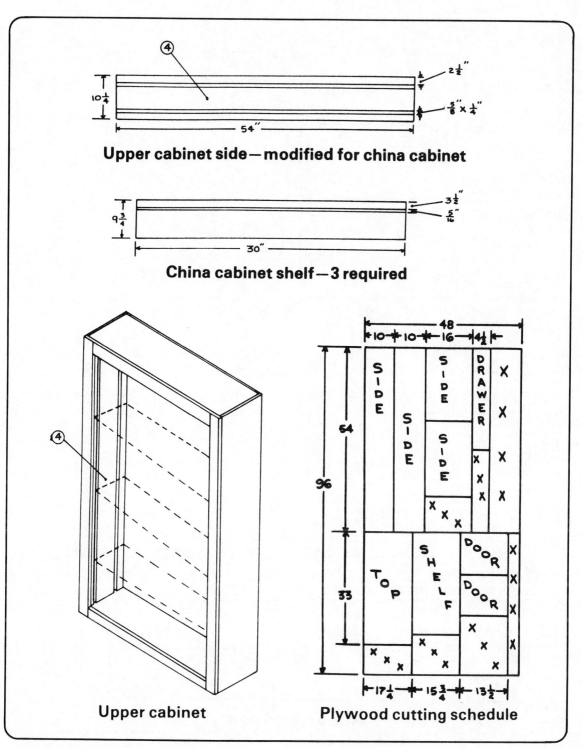

④

$2\frac{1}{2}"$

$10\frac{1}{4}$

$\frac{1}{4}"$

$\frac{5}{8}" \times \frac{1}{4}"$

54"

Upper cabinet side—modified for china cabinet

$3\frac{1}{2}"$

$\frac{5}{16}"$

$9\frac{3}{4}$

30"

China cabinet shelf—3 required

④

Upper cabinet

48

10 10 16 $4\frac{1}{2}$

96

54

33

SIDE SIDE SIDE DRAWER X

SIDE X

X

X X X

X X X

SHELF DOOR X

TOP DOOR X

X X

X X X X X X

$17\frac{1}{4}$ $15\frac{3}{4}$ $13\frac{1}{2}$

Plywood cutting schedule

Construction details for cabinet.

81

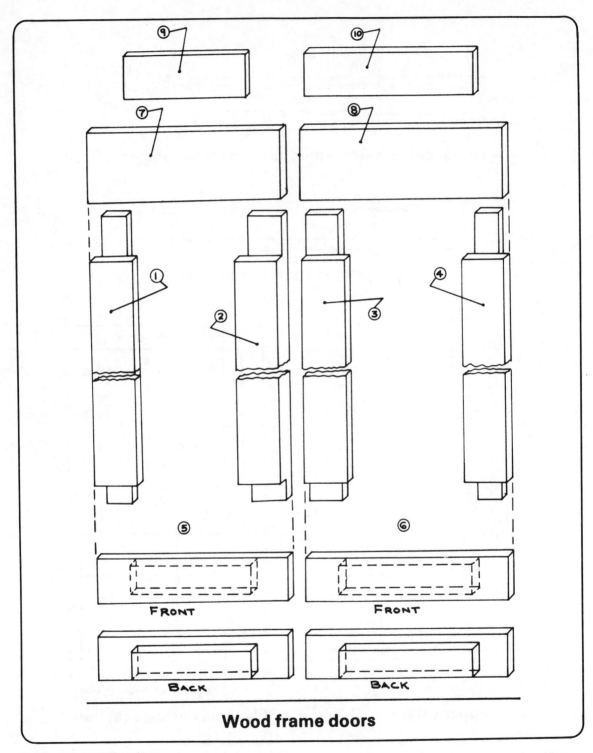

Wood frame doors

Construction details for cabinet.

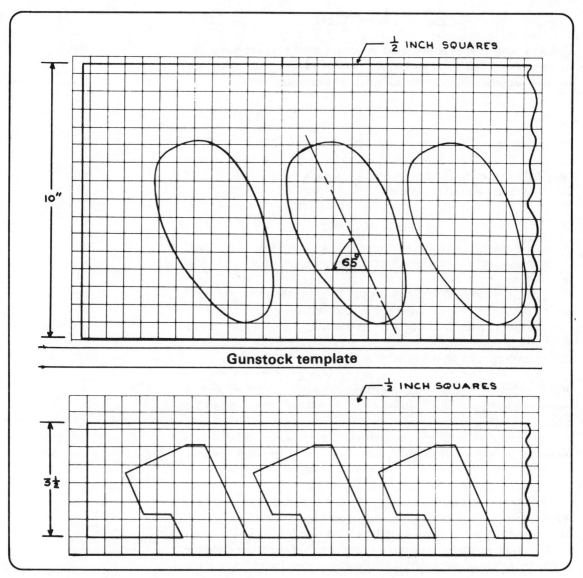

22: Ladder

Ladders are a rather expensive item, but a must-have for homeowners. Why not make your own and put your more advanced woodworking skills to work at the same time?

* * *

Basswood was chosen for this project because it lends itself to this type of construction quite well, is fairly inexpensive, and is easy to work with. However, similar woods such as pine or fir could be substituted if desired.

CONSTRUCTION

Construction is basically simple but depends on a great deal of accuracy. To eliminate human error, use jigs, patterns, and templates.

First, rip the front stringers (no. 1 in drawing). Use a template to cut the angles on the top and bottom.

Cut steps (no. 2) using a template and a stop block setup on the table saw. This eliminates any error due to carelessness. Cut chamfers on the steps with a miter box saw and jig.

Cut three 1/4-inch dadoes in the stringers to receive the steps, using the dado attachment on the table saw. Use a stop block setup to cut the dadoes also, to assure they will all be equal.

The last operation on the stringers is to locate and drill the holes for assembly. First, drill holes in the stringer sides where the steps are to be fastened on the drill press, with the use of a precut template.

The braces for the top (no. 3) were cut from 3/8-inch stock. Again, use a template. In addition to drilling three holes for the screws, a 5/16-inch hole was drilled. This was for a 1/4 × 2-inch carriage bolt which was used later for fastening the front stringer and the back legs. When the braces were completed, they were assembled to the front stringers.

Rip out and cut the back legs (no. 4) to length in much the same way as the front stringers. The 5/16-inch holes have to be drilled for carriage bolts. Use a template to drill precisely.

Cut two back cross slats and one horizontal slat from 3/8-inch stock to a rough length (nos. 5 and 6). After they are assembled on the back legs, cut them off evenly. To assemble the slats, lay out and nail the back legs on a simple jig holding device. This assures that all back legs will be the same.

The "pail holder" (for a lack of a better name) is easily constructed.

Cut out the arms (no. 7) and drill two 5/16-inch holes into them. A simple cardboard template gives accuracy and uniformity. Cut out the 1/4-inch plywood shelf (no. 8). Assemble the shelf and arms using two-penny nails. Following the assembly, rough sand the sides for neatness.

A piece of 1/16 × 1/2 × 5 1/2-inch band iron is used for a brace and hinge combined (no. 9). First, cut it to a rough length of 5 3/4 inch and grind on the grinder to smooth out and round the edges. Then lay out and drill for the bolts and screws.

Cut the top step (no. 10) to size, again using a stop block setup on the table saw. Edge the step with a portable router. Grooves in the top step (in this case) were made on the drill press using a router bit attachment. A total of six 1/4-inch grooves were made on each piece.

ASSEMBLY

To assemble the ladder (refer to drawing), first put together the steps and stringers, then fasten the top braces to the top of the stringer. Next assemble the back legs. The ladder pivots (opens and closes) on a 1/4 × 2-inch carriage bolt.

Fasten the band iron to the arms of the "pail holder" with 1/4 × 1 1/2-inch carriage bolts. Follow by fastening the whole thing to the back legs of the ladder with 1/4 × 2 1/2-inch carriage bolts. Turn ladders upside down and use screws to fasten the other end of the band iron to the inside of the front stringer.

The last step is assembling the top to the ladder. For this use four 2-inch box nails.

Because individual pieces are sanded during construction, there is not too much final sanding to do. Also, due to the nature of a step ladder, finishing techniques are not greatly emphasized. Ladders can be given a coat of shellac followed by one coat of brushing lacquer. If desired, you can apply spray lacquer to the ladders.

Materials

Pcs.	Description	Size (inches)	Material
2	front stringer	3/4 × 2 1/2 × 47	basswood
3	steps	3/4 × 3 1/2 × 14	basswood
4	braces	3/8 × 2 1/4 × 6 3/4	basswood
2	back legs	3/4 × 1 3/4 × 45	basswood
2	cross slats	3/8 × 1 1/8 × 30	basswood
1	horiz. slat	3/8 × 1 1/8 × 14 3/4	basswood
2	pail-holder arms	3/4 × 1 1/8 × 17 1/2	basswood
1	pail-holder shelf	1/4 × 8 × 12 3/4	fir plywood
2	reinforcements and hinges	1/16 × 1/2 × 5 1/2	band iron
1	top step	3/4 × 5 1/2 × 17 1/2	basswood
14	screws	3/4 #8 rh	steel
12	screws	1 1/2 #8 rh	steel
2	carriage bolts	1/4 × 1 1/2	steel
2	carriage bolts	1/4 × 2	steel
2	carriage bolts	1/4 × 2 1/2	steel

Materials list for ladder.

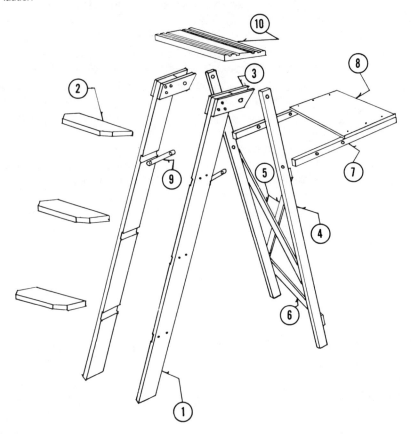

Exploded view of ladder.

Part Three

Projects Using

Special Techniques and Tools

The more tools you gain experience with, the wider you're wood-working horizons will be. This section offers projects involving the use of specific tools and operations: woodturning, woodcarving, jigs, the lathe, the bandsaw, and even laminating and bending wood.

23: Salt Shaker/Pepper Mill Using Wood-Turning Operations

Are you new to the idea of woodturning? Or have you tried it and had problems? Making a simple project such as this salt shaker/pepper mill set can teach you how painlessly.

* * *

Construction failure frequently frustrates efforts to pursue the fashioning of matching pepper mills and salt shakers and similar projects requiring wood turning. Loss of lineup in disassembling the work before it is completed is the most common cause of construction failure—and yet this frustration can easily be avoided.

Because the successful construction of the pepper mills and salt shakers depends on aligning a true vertical hole between thin side walls, avoid simple spindle-turning followed by boring at a drill press. Bore first . . . and at a lathe with a tapered chuck and the necessary multispur drills attached to the live spindle. Attach a spur-center to the dead end and feed the work at slow speed.

Use a longer-than-necessary stock to prevent striking the drill. Maintain a drilling order to permit the drilling of the larger holes first and leave a center for smaller drills to penetrate.

Turn two tapered hardwood plugs to fit each end of the hollow stock. Trim the stock to no more than 1/8 inch above finished length.

If turning is begun next, it could result in some sections of

Finished salt and pepper shakers.

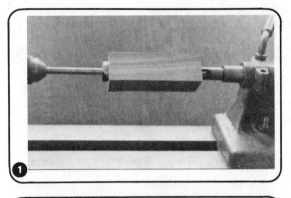

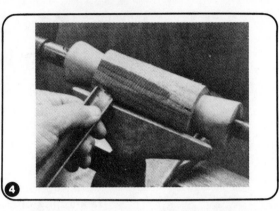

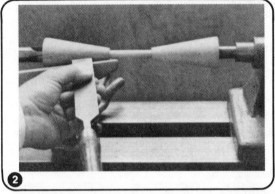

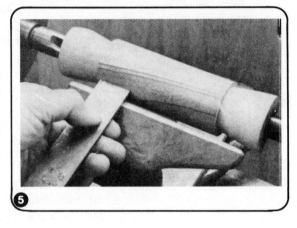

Steps to woodturning. 1) the initial boring. 2) Balancing the mandrel. 3) The stock, trimmed to length and assembled for turning. 4) the roughing-in operation. 5) Smoothing the stock. After this stage, you may begin implementing your own design variations.

the side walls becoming too thin since the cutting tools can force the work out of line. To prevent this, use a large-diameter dowel to connect the smaller ends of the tapered plugs.

To assure alignment, bore the smaller ends of the plugs at the lathe.

Before fitting the project, assemble the plugs with the connecting dowel and true-up the tapered surfaces; then the work may be turned. If necessary, the whole setup may be removed and reassembled with little loss of lineup.

24: Capture the
Beauty of Woodcarving

By incorporating woodcarving techniques in your woodworking projects, you introduce a whole new artistic and creative dimension to your projects.

* * *

Somehow the average person typically conceives of woodcarving as an artistic portrayal of human, animal, or abstract form. Instead of interpreting woodcarving from a strictly esthetic viewpoint, why not combine both beauty and utility in the form of decorative woodenware? The creative design possibilities in this vast area are unlimited, including such attractive articles as serving trays, chip-and-dip trays, salad bowls, candy trays, and salad servers. The illustrated candy tray is intended primarily as an example that typifies simplicity of line and form.

In planning the design, utilize free-flowing lines and graceful contours. An interesting effect can be gained by varying the thickness of the edge, thereby creating slightly different shapes for the interior and exterior contours of the tray.

Lay out the top view on the stock. The beauty of the tray can be greatly enhanced by utilizing the grain pattern to its fullest extent. If a burl or other unusual figured piece of stock is availa-

Woodcarving teaches basic design principles of line and form.

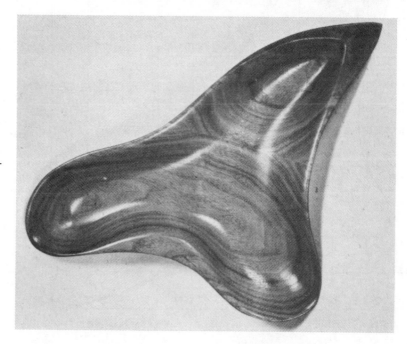

ble, it might be appropriate to actually design the tray to fully utilize such grain configurations.

Cut a shallow "ditch" along the inside of the tray edge with an inside gouge. This ditch cut is necessary in order to prevent splintering of the tray edge as the rough stock in the tray interior is removed. Using an outside gouge and mallet, rough out the tray interior. Deep bowls and trays might require the use of several sizes of bent shank gouges. After completing the roughing operation, pare the inside of the tray to its final shape. Continue smoothing the interior with rotary files and bent riffler files.

Sand the interior with garnet sandpaper, working down to 7/0. Cut the exterior of the tray on the band saw. In order to gain an attractive receding sidewall, set the saw at an angle of 30 to 45 degrees. Shape the tray exterior with contour sanders; do the final shaping with surform and bent riffler files. Sand the tray exterior and apply a wipe-on finish that is resistant to food oils.

This candy dish is just a sample of the many forms a wood-carving can take. The coloration, grain, texture, and simplicity of line all combine to result in a handsome, graceful article.

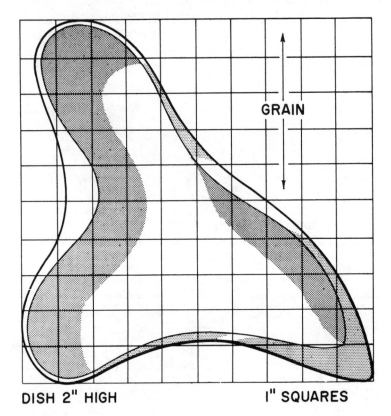

GRAIN

Designing the carving;
gracefully round the lip.

DISH 2" HIGH   I" SQUARES

25: Make Your Own Picture Frame from a Shop-Built Jig

Picture frames are items very much in demand, and are rather expensive as well. Here are the basic instructions. Why not use special finishes or even woodcarving to make a beautiful and unique finished product?

* * *

Constructing a picture frame will help you develop craftsmanship and gain experience in precise measuring. Using commercial frame molding, however, can be expensive and wasteful. As an alternative you can make a simple jig to use on a thickness planer for making your own beveled picture frame molding from 3/4-inch stock.

To make the jig, you need two pieces of stock. The first (A) is 2 x 6 inches and the length of your planer table. The second piece (B) can be any size, but it must be square, fit over the front edge of the planer infeed table, and be perpendicular to A.

To cut the notch in A, tilt the blade of the circular saw to 10 degrees and adjust the height of the blade to correspond to the desired thickness of your molding (mine is 3/4 inch) minus 1/16 inch. (*Note:* use caution when cutting the notch.)

Make the first pass on the face of A. To finish the notch, adjust the height of the circular saw blade and adjust the rip fence, leaving the blade at 10 degrees, and align the blade to complete the cut. This is the dangerous part because the blade is adjusted to near maximum height.

Using wood screws and glue, secure A and B together, making certain the two are exactly perpendicular. Keep in mind that the degree of the circular saw blade may be changed if more or less bevel is desired.

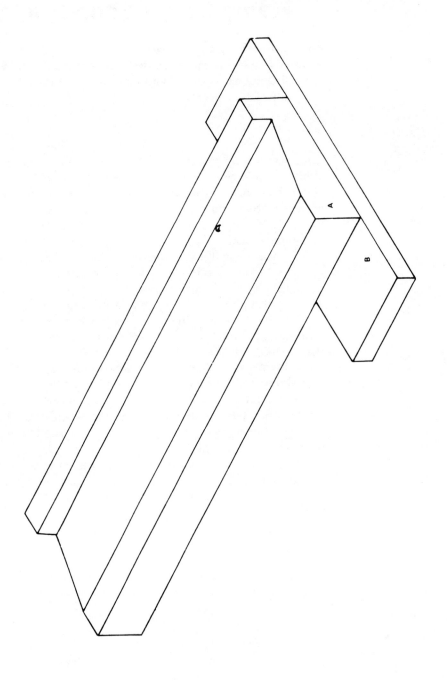

Picture frame jig.

Feed the stock into the thickness planer with the frame molding jig in place.

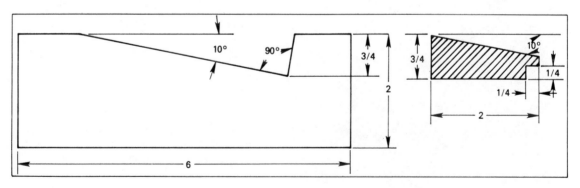

End view (left) and section finished molding (right).

95

26: Cedar Post Turnings on the Lathe

Planning to learn to use a lathe? Here is an introductory project to teach you basic skills for use with this versatile tool. Cedar post turnings will spark your creativity; many different projects can be made. Posts are available from lumber yards, co-ops, etc., and are relatively inexpensive.

* * *

A number of projects are possible.

PROCEDURE

1. Decide on the shape and type of turning. A rough sketch or half template should be sufficient. Projects could include vases for dried flower arrangements, candle holders, and lamp bases.

2. Cut off a section of the post about 1 inch longer than the pattern. This allows for cutting flat ends on the turning. A buck saw makes cutting easier.

3. Set up the post between lathe spindles. Large protruding knots should be trimmed off to make rough turning easier.

4. Turn to shape, using the pattern, and cut the bottom flat. No sanding is necessary.

5. Remove the project from the lathe; cut off excess. Drill holes if required.

6. Char the piece, including top and bottom, with a propane torch.

7. Wire brush the project until the charred layer is removed. An electric hand drill with a wire brush attachment works well. This removes the soft wood, accentuating the harder portions of the grain and giving an interesting effect.

8. Stain with a dark oil-base stain, if desired.

9. Apply one or two coats of paste wax and the project is completed.

Cedar post turning starts at the lathe with a rough post set in between spindles.

27: Turned Tables

You will find many beautiful projects using lathe procedures. After you've gained some skills try these tables. They are made almost entirely on the wood lathe.

* * *

TABLE 1

A scaled-down version of a larger table inspired this miniature turned table. This is a project you will want to add in the wood-turning area. It is not only a decorative piece, but can also be used as a table for potted flowers, a lamp table, a smoking stand, and as a table for serving refreshments.

The table will give the wood turner an opportunity to develop or further expand and refine skills because both spindle and faceplate turnings are involved. The cost, depending on the

A completed miniature turned table 1.

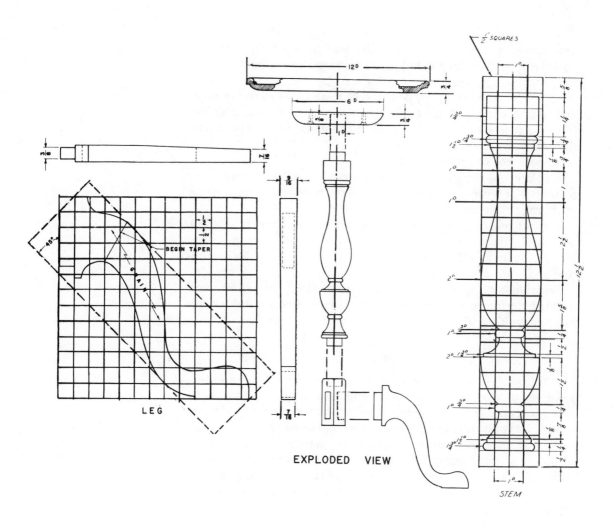

EXPLODED VIEW

STEM

LEG

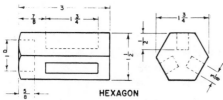

HEXAGON

Materials		
No. of Pieces	Name of Part	Size
1	Stem	2 × 2 × 12 1/2
1	Top	12 × 12 × 3/4
1	Top Support	6 × 6 × 3/4
1	Hexagon	3 × 1 3/4 × 1 1/2
3	Legs	3 × 3 3/4 × 9/16

Materials list and construction details for miniature turned table 1.

wood selected, is not great because less than 3 board feet are used. Any of the finer cabinet-grade hardwoods, such as mahogany, walnut, cherry, or korina, can be used with excellent results. The small quantity of wood required makes this project well worth the small material cost when it is realized that the finished product will have increased the value of the raw material about 15 times.

Some construction hints:

To prevent cupping, the top of the table should be made from a number of narrow—2-inch wide—pieces of stock, reversing the end grain direction.

When making the hexagon, process the stock to 1 1/2-x-1 3/4-inch. The rectangular stock should be processed in longer pieces, such as three or four units of 3 1/4-inch, for safety reasons.

The finish applied to the table depends on the wood used and the desired color. Excellent results have been obtained using penetrating oil and various film (surface) finishes.

TABLE 2

This table will allow you to refine your turning techniques, because it involves inside and plug chucking in addition to faceplate and spindle turnings. Such fine cabinet-grade hardwoods as walnut, cherry, mahogany, and butternut have been used with excellent results. The naturally darker colored woods, or darker stained woods, will show up and emphasize the brass trim and the stem and legs. The ratio of raw material cost to a finished product value is quite high, thus making it an appealing project.

Construction

In gluing up stock for the top, to prevent cupping, use a number of narrow (2-inch wide) pieces and reverse grain directions. The rough top can be planed to the approximate finished thickness. After laying out the diameter, the top should be cut to about 1/4-inch oversize on the band saw. A large faceplate can then be mounted on the lathe, using care to be accurate. The top can then be mounted and turned to the desired diameter and shape. After the top has been sanded smooth, all coats of finish and waxcan be applied while it is still on the lathe.

Making the top support piece involves the same layout procedures and work operations on the lathe plus using the lathe tailstock to bore the hole for the top stem tenon. In making the stem, it is best to develop a full-size pattern and prepare square stock to about 1/4-inch oversize. The ends of the stem must be turned accurately to snugly fit the bored hole and the brass tubing at the lower end.

Making the hexagon shape at the center of the base and tapering the edges and faces of the legs introduce different problems of layout and work operations for the students so that the table is an excellent vehicle for learning a wide range of layout and work techniques. Again, accuracy is important in boring the hole for the bottom stem tenon and in cutting and fitting tenons and mortises to fit the legs to the hexagon.

In assembling the finished parts, the stem should be glued to the base subassembly with the brass tubing in position. Then check carefully for levelness while gluing the top support piece to the stem and base assembly. The top can be fastened to the top support piece with screws. The finish will vary, of course, with the kind of wood used and with the desires of the individual: A better job usually results if the finish is applied and rubbed down while the parts are rotating.

Materials

Part Name	Quantity	Dimensions
Top	1	1" × 19" × 19"
Top support	1	1" × 9" × 9"
Stem	1	2-1/2" × 2-1/2" × 19-3/4"
Hexagon	1	2-1/8" × 2-1/2" × 3-1/2"
Legs	3	1-1/8" × 2-3/8" × 8-1/8"
Plugs for ferrules	3	1" × 1" × 1-3/8"
Brass ferrules	3	Trim open (top) end to 3/4" length
Seamless brass tubing	1	2" ID × 3-1/2" long

Materials list and table 2.

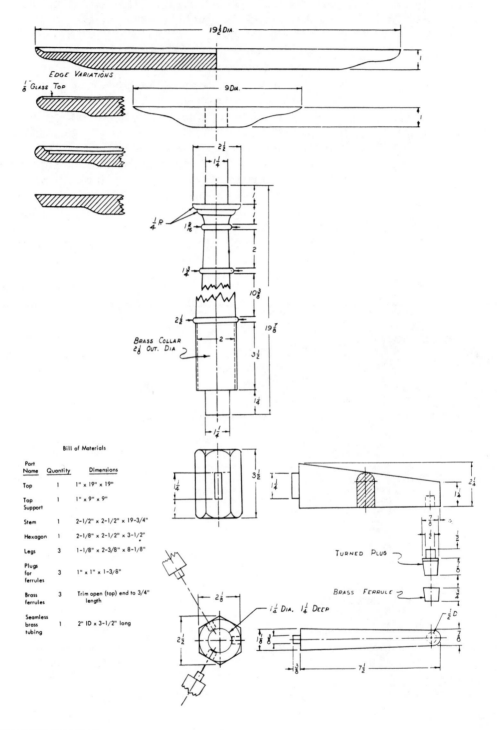

$19\frac{1}{2}$ DIA.

EDGE VARIATIONS

$\frac{1}{8}$" GLASS TOP

9 DIA.

$2\frac{1}{2}$

$1\frac{1}{4}$

$\frac{1}{4}$ R

$1\frac{9}{16}$

2

$1\frac{3}{4}$

$10\frac{3}{8}$

$2\frac{1}{2}$

$19\frac{7}{8}$

BRASS COLLAR
$2\frac{1}{8}$ OUT. DIA

2

$3\frac{1}{2}$

$1\frac{1}{4}$

$1\frac{1}{4}$

Bill of Materials

Part Name	Quantity	Dimensions
Top	1	1" x 19" x 19"
Top Support	1	1" x 9" x 9"
Stem	1	2-1/2" x 2-1/2" x 19-3/4"
Hexagon	1	2-1/8" x 2-1/2" x 3-1/2"
Legs	3	1-1/8" x 2-3/8" x 8-1/8"
Plugs for ferrules	3	1" x 1" x 1-3/8"
Brass ferrules	3	Trim open (top) end to 3/4" length
Seamless brass tubing	1	2" ID x 3-1/2" long

$3\frac{1}{2}$

$1\frac{1}{4}$

$1\frac{1}{4}$

$2\frac{1}{4}$

$1\frac{1}{4}$

TURNED PLUG

$\frac{7}{8}$

$\frac{1}{2}$

$\frac{1}{2}$

$\frac{3}{8}$

BRASS FERRULE

$\frac{3}{4}$

$1\frac{1}{4}$ DIA. $1\frac{1}{4}$ DEEP

$2\frac{1}{8}$

$2\frac{1}{2}$

$1\frac{3}{8}$

$\frac{3}{8}$

$7\frac{1}{2}$

$\frac{1}{2}$ D

$\frac{7}{8}$

Construction details for table 2.

102

28: Laminating and Bending Wood for a Chair

A number of different tools and techniques are involved in this project: put your skills and creativity to work!

* * *

Some good reasons for attempting this method of construction follow:

1. It offers a different method for fabricating a product.
2. Members can be made much stronger with less weight and size.
3. It offers unlimited opportunities for creative design.
4. It offers a challenge.
5. In many cases it saves on material.

Lamination is the process of gluing two or more pieces of wood with the grain running in the same direction. Bent lamination is the process of applying glue to the surface of two or more layers of wood, then placing them in a fixture that causes them to conform to a pre-determined curve, or curves, and applying pressure until the glue has set.

After a chair was selected as the project, many free-hand sketches were made in an attempt to create an acceptable design. From the drawings, a mock-up of the chair was made to study the overall appearance and make necessary changes in design. For the mock-up, 1/16-inch welding rod was bent into the shape of the members and cardboard was taped to the welding rod to give a three-dimensional effect.

The next step in developing the chair was designing and building the molds to produce the desired results. This was one of the major problem-solving aspects in building the project. The type of molds, clamping methods, and type of material used for building molds will vary for different kinds of bends. Other factors may be the amount of money and type of equipment available for producing the molds.

A male-female type mold was used for the back. Because much pressure had to be exerted on the mold during clamping, a hardwood was chosen. A Masonite pattern was made to design both sections of the mold.

In designing the male-female type mold, the two molds must be concentric to each other. This will depend on the number and thickness of the veneers used. It is important to have both sections of the mold machined very accurately to produce good glue joints on the glued member.

Because of the machine limitations in our shop, the molds were made in sections, shaped, and glued with aligning pins. Aligning bars were installed so the female mold would come down in the correct position on the male part of the mold.

Clamping bars, placed across the top of the mold, pulled the two sections together. Some type of press could also be used to apply pressure on the molds. A foam-rubber gasket was used to take up the small irregularities in the molds and veneers during the gluing process.

A different style mold was used for the legs, arms, and back support. For these members, molds with bands and cauls were used. The molds were built up of 3/4-inch plywood and covered with Masonite. After the molds were cut on the bandsaw, they were accurately shaped on a large disc sander. Sections of the molds were cut out to allow room for the cauls and clamping.

It was necessary to fasten hardwood bases to the molds to withstand the clamping pressure of the bands. A 28-gage stainless steel band was selected to pull the veneers around the mold. Use some material such as stainless steel, which has a high tensile strength, because the pull on the band is very great. Wooden cauls were installed at the points where there was no pressure from the band. The cauls were made of oak, reinforced with steel straps. Wheel pullers were used to pull the cauls down on the veneers.

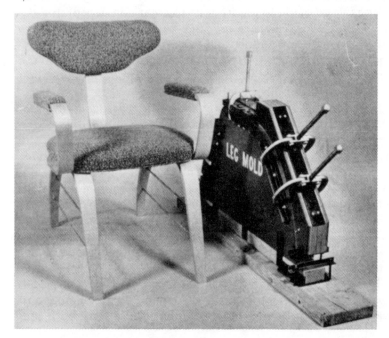

A chair from laminated and bent wood (left) and leg mold (right).

Leg mold and arm-and-back-support mold with their parts marked.

A urea resin glue, recommended for lamination, was used to glue all the members.

Another problem to be solved was distortion. The first members, after removal from the molds, distorted out of shape. All of the possible causes of distortion will not be listed here, but such things as arrangement of the grain pattern of the veneers, glue mixture, assembly periods, and length of curing were all factors that must be taken into consideration.

Shrinkage was also a problem. After the members are removed from the molds, they become smaller. One of the causes seems to be the water in the glue, which effects the moisture content in the veneers during gluing and curing periods. The glue-water ratio was controlled as accurately as possible to the 1/10 of a gram to allow for equal shrinkage of all the members.

After the members were allowed to cure for approximately 24 hours, the glue squeeze-out was trimmed off with a saber saw and hand plane. Safety goggles were worn during the trimming operations because of the danger from flying pieces of the hard urea resin adhesive. The members were cut to size and shaped by using a combination of operations on the jointer, circle saw, band saw, and saber saw. Special machine guards were built for some operations because of the curvilinear shape of the members. It was also necessary to design and build special jigs and fixtures to hold some members for making special cuts.

The 3/8-inch plated rods are pinned into the legs. Their main purpose is to strengthen the legs, but they also add to the appearance of the chair. Button-head cap screws hold the legs, arms, and back support to the 3/4-inch plywood seat. The nuts for the button-head cap screws were set flush with the top side of the seat before the upholstery was applied. The arms, legs, and back support can be disassembled from the seat at any time.

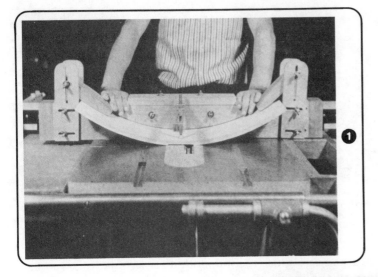

1) Cutting the back dado with a special jig.

2) A male-female mold used for the back which requires accurate machining.

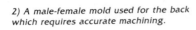
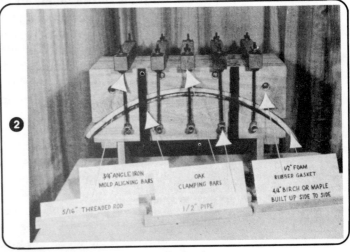

3/4" ANGLE IRON
MOLD ALIGNING BARS

OAK
CLAMPING BARS

1/2" FOAM
RUBBER GASKET

4/4" BIRCH OR MAPLE
BUILT UP SIDE TO SIDE

5/16" THREADED ROD

1/2" PIPE

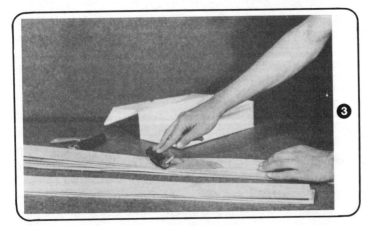

3) Applying glue with a rubber roller to provide a uniform coating for lamination.

106

29: Cutting Perfect Circles Using a Bandsaw Jig

The bandsaw is an invaluable piece of woodshop equipment. Inexperienced and experienced woodworkers alike, however, might find cutting circular parts a challenge. Here's how to make perfect circles every time, using a jig.

* * *

Producing circular parts can present production problems. But this bandsaw jig, designed to position itself firmly and accurately in place every time, will produce perfect circles. The sliding table with multiple center locations allows circles of many diameters to be cut quickly and accurately with little finishing work necessary.

Here's how it works: Center drill the blank workpiece to fit over the adjustable pivot pin in the sliding table. Then, with the bandsaw running, feed the blank into the blade by sliding the table forward as far as it will go, making sure the workpiece does not move. Now rotate the workpiece; the pivot pin guides it as you turn.

The key to successful jig operation is the location of the pivot guide pin and its relationship to the front edge of the bandsaw blade. The center line of the pivot pin holes must cross align exactly with the front (cutting side) of the bandsaw blade. If the blade wanders from this position, a broken blade or an imperfect circle will result.

MAKING THE JIG

1. Cut a base larger than the bandsaw table. Base width depends on the number of pivot holes desired.

2. Attach side strips to underside of base. Strips must be the width of the table apart. Glue and screw in place.

3. Move base into moving saw blade to cut the saw kerf. Move forward until base clears the front edge of table by 1 inch.

4. Glue front and back positioning strips to base underside. Distance between strips should equal the length of the table. Base assembly should fit snug.

5. After glue sets, cut blade kerf through front strip using a backsaw. Remove base assembly and add screws through base into front and back strips.

6. Place base-strip assembly on bandsaw table top. Assembly should fit snug with no forward or side play.

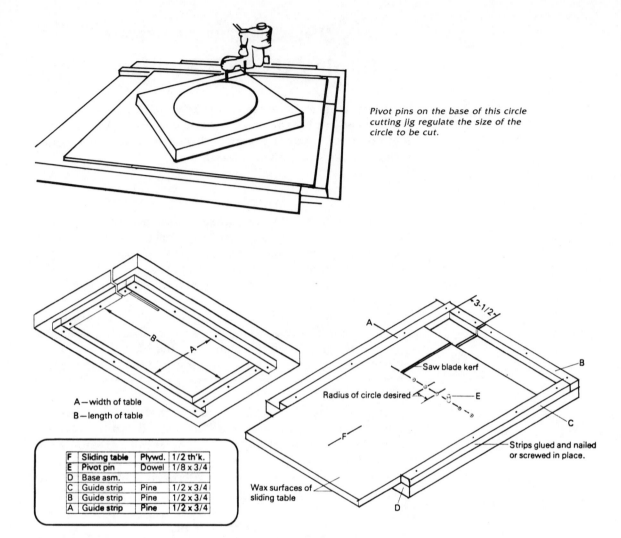

Pivot pins on the base of this circle cutting jig regulate the size of the circle to be cut.

A—width of table
B—length of table

Saw blade kerf

Radius of circle desired

E

Strips glued and nailed or screwed in place.

Wax surfaces of sliding table

F	Sliding table	Plywd.	1/2 th'k.
E	Pivot pin	Dowel	1/8 x 3/4
D	Base asm.		
C	Guide strip	Pine	1/2 x 3/4
B	Guide strip	Pine	1/2 x 3/4
A	Guide strip	Pine	1/2 x 3/4

7. Refer to second figure. Position guide strip A on base assembly; secure with glue and screws. Strip must be parallel to blade kerf. Guide strips must be the same thickness or smaller than the sliding table.

8. Cut the sliding table to required size. Holding table firmly against guide strip, slide it into moving blade to cut blade kerf.

9. Position guide strip B at front of base assembly. Glue and screw in place. Position guide strip C. Table should slide freely against all guide strips.

10. With sliding table in position, construct a line perpendicular to the front of blade. Layout pivot pin hole locations on line equal to the radius of circles required. Drill holes and insert pivot pin. Jig is ready for use.

Base positioning strip assembly, bottom view (left). Circle cutting jig assembly complete (right).

30: Constructing a Chess board

This is a more complicated project, but the time and effort are worth it—the end result is beautiful.

* * *

Most of the boards for this chessboard are made from solid wood strips or squares. Many suffer from misalignment, warpage, and separation of glue joints. These problems can be eliminated without sacrificing any of the beauty of the finished piece.

The secret is to laminate fancy-faced 1/8-inch plywood in 2- x -2-inch squares to a thick plywood base. Because the base can be any size, different fancy borders can be added or even a table top made, without losing any structural integrity.

Special jigs are used as in the third figure to cut the plywood squares accurately. Push handles are designed to accommodate 2-inch squares.

The only challenge in making the cutting jig is to assure that the permanent guide fence is set parallel to and accurately from the saw blade. Use an 18-gauge thin rim blade for cutting. Because the guard cannot be used in this cutting operation, take care whenever the blade is turning, even though it will only protrude a maximum of 1/4-inch above the jig surface.

Set the blade just high enough to cut the material. Feed the plywood through the jig to make long strips. Using the push handle, cut the strips into squares. By choosing the best face of your material first and by setting the blade properly, you can keep splintering to a minimum.

ASSEMBLY

Construct the assembly jig carefully, following the sixth figure, so that it firmly holds eight rows of eight squares each.

Assemble the squares with their good faces up, alternating light and dark. Check that the grain of all light squares runs perpendicular to the grain of all dark squares. As each horizontal row is completed, tape it with 3/4-inch masking tape. When all rows are taped horizontally, tape each row vertically.

When all 64 squares are securely taped in both directions, push the assembly from the jig. The squares will remain held together by the tape.

Cut a piece of 5/8-inch plywood for the base. You might also use particleboard. If you are making just the basic board, cut the base 1/2-inch larger than the assembled squares. Square two of the adjoining edges of the base and mark these edges.

Quantity	Size	Description
	Materials	
1	16 × 16 × 5/8-in.	plywood
32	2 × 2 × 1/8-in.	plywood (fancy light)
32	2 × 2 × 1/8-in.	plywood (fancy dark)
8	1/4 × 3/4 × 17-in.	border strips (4 light, 4 dark)
1	17 × 17-in.	felt

Materials list for chess set.

Coat the underside of the taped squares and the surface of the base with contact cement. When both surfaces are ready, carefully place the squares on the base so they are aligned with the marked base edges. Kraft paper or wood strips will help alignment. After rolling or pounding the surface to assure complete adhesion, remove the masking tape from the squares.

BORDERS

Using solid woods to match the shades of the squares, cut border strips exactly 1/4-inch thick. A 3/4-inch width will allow for trimming after assembly. Glue these strips together, one light and one dark. You can clamp four sets together at once.

Miter and attach the border strips to the assembled board. When the glue has set, hand plane or scrape the border to make it even with the surface and bottom of the board.

SANDING AND FINISHING

A good sanding process is absolutely essential to a perfect finish. Each square should be individually sanded; a good orbital sander, however, won't leave any noticeable surface marks.

If you should damage a square, it can be easily lifted out and replaced. Using a wide, sharp chisel, bevel down, cut through the square and pry it out. It should lift out without damaging any other square.

Finish your chessboard with any standard process. Spray lacquer is especially effective. When the finish is dry, cover the bottom of the board with a piece of felt.

VARIATIONS

There is no limit to the variations one can make on the existing board. The board can even be incorporated into a table.

A variety of borders can enhance the appearance of the basic board. These can range from a simple hardwood or veneer mitered border to fancy marquetry (inlay) designs.

The push handle makes cutting perfect squares a snap. A little care will prevent splintering of delicate veneer.

A particularly popular border uses 1/2-inch squares to make a mosaic pattern. By making a cutting jig and push handle for this size square, the components can be made and assembled the same as the larger squares. The sixth figure shows how to make an assembly jig. A block of wood slightly less than 2 inches wide is used to tap the squares firmly together. These squares are taped in place as the larger squares were.

Curring jig is easily constructed and will last a long time. Permanent guides ride in table saw grooves.

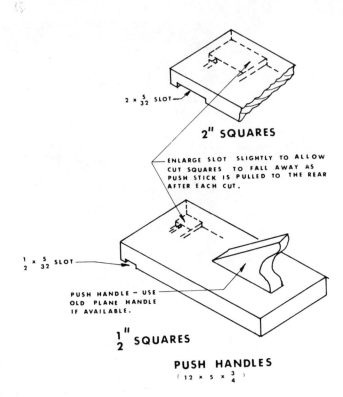

$2 \times \frac{5}{32}$ SLOT

2" SQUARES

ENLARGE SLOT SLIGHTLY TO ALLOW
CUT SQUARES TO FALL AWAY AS
PUSH STICK IS PULLED TO THE REAR
AFTER EACH CUT.

$\frac{1}{2} \times \frac{5}{32}$ SLOT

PUSH HANDLE — USE
OLD PLANE HANDLE
IF AVAILABLE.

$\frac{1}{2}$" SQUARES

PUSH HANDLES
($12 \times 5 \times \frac{3}{4}$)

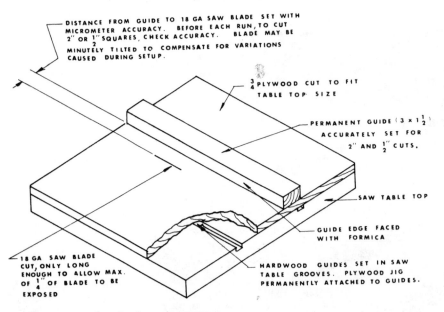

DISTANCE FROM GUIDE TO 18 GA SAW BLADE SET WITH
MICROMETER ACCURACY. BEFORE EACH RUN, TO CUT
2" OR $1\frac{1}{2}$" SQUARES, CHECK ACCURACY. BLADE MAY BE
MINUTELY TILTED TO COMPENSATE FOR VARIATIONS
CAUSED DURING SETUP.

$\frac{3}{4}$ PLYWOOD CUT TO FIT
TABLE TOP SIZE

PERMANENT GUIDE ($3 \times 1\frac{1}{2}$)
ACCURATELY SET FOR
2" AND $\frac{1}{2}$" CUTS.

SAW TABLE TOP

GUIDE EDGE FACED
WITH FORMICA

18 GA SAW BLADE
CUT, ONLY LONG
ENOUGH TO ALLOW MAX.
OF $\frac{1}{4}$" OF BLADE TO BE
EXPOSED

HARDWOOD GUIDES SET IN SAW
TABLE GROOVES. PLYWOOD JIG
PERMANENTLY ATTACHED TO GUIDES.

Jigs for cutting chessboard and mosaic squares.

112

Squares are held firmly in place by precision jig, then taped down. Alternate grain as well as color.

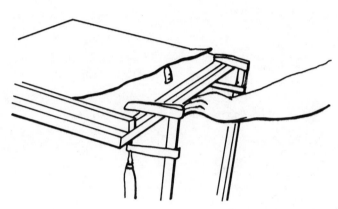

When all squares are secured with tape, the surface can be lifted from the jig by poking through a hole.

Plywood base is cut slightly oversize. Board is laminated along two squared sides. Wood strips help positioning.

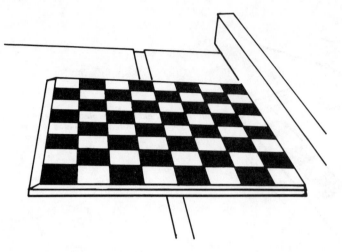

The two unsquared surfaces of the plywood are trimmed off. The result is a firm, integrated, non-warping chessboard.

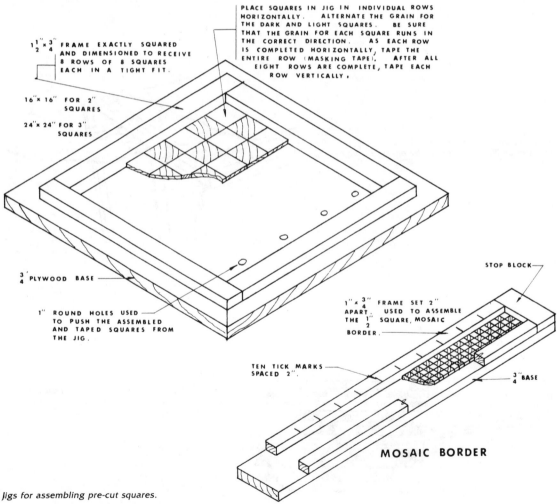

$1\frac{1}{2}'' \times \frac{3}{4}''$ FRAME EXACTLY SQUARED AND DIMENSIONED TO RECEIVE 8 ROWS OF 8 SQUARES EACH IN A TIGHT FIT.

16" x 16" FOR 2" SQUARES

24" x 24" FOR 3" SQUARES

PLACE SQUARES IN JIG IN INDIVIDUAL ROWS HORIZONTALLY. ALTERNATE THE GRAIN FOR THE DARK AND LIGHT SQUARES. BE SURE THAT THE GRAIN FOR EACH SQUARE RUNS IN THE CORRECT DIRECTION. AS EACH ROW IS COMPLETED HORIZONTALLY, TAPE THE ENTIRE ROW (MASKING TAPE). AFTER ALL EIGHT ROWS ARE COMPLETE, TAPE EACH ROW VERTICALLY.

$\frac{3}{4}''$ PLYWOOD BASE

1" ROUND HOLES USED TO PUSH THE ASSEMBLED AND TAPED SQUARES FROM THE JIG.

STOP BLOCK

$1'' \times \frac{3}{4}''$ FRAME SET 2" APART. USED TO ASSEMBLE THE $\frac{1}{2}''$ SQUARE, MOSAIC BORDER.

TEN TICK MARKS SPACED 2".

$\frac{3}{4}''$ BASE

MOSAIC BORDER

Jigs for assembling pre-cut squares.

Finished chessboard.

Chessboard used as a table top.

The key to assembling the mosaic strips is to make all the lines formed by the large and small squares continuous. Alignment is achieved by adjusting as necessary during the dry fitting process.

Part Four
Projects with Special Additions

Knowing how to work with materials other than wood means endless creative possibilities. Instead of making a wooden footstool, make an upholstered wooden footstool. Add an interesting touch to a table with ceramic mosaic inlay. Wooden bowls are beautiful, wooden bowls with metal bases have a beauty all their own.

These are the projects in this part and are but a few suggestions for special additions to your fine woodworking—there are hundreds more.

31: Upholstered Footstool

Add a new dimension to your woodworking by trying your hand at upholstery. These footstools add a decorative touch to any home and make perfect gifts.

* * *

Three popular footstool styles are colonial, Queen Anne, and contemporary. Many of the procedures involved in these styles can be applied to other footstool designs, both in construction, and upholstery.

MATERIALS

Needed materials can be bought in local upholstery shops. Foam rubber padding is a good selection because it is easy to hold in place and it allows a smooth surface on the finished seat—but horse hair, moss, and cotton are also acceptable. A 3-ounce steel upholstering tack is recommended for most footstool work.

For covering, needlepoint or small pattern tapestry is recommended for the colonial or Queen Anne, and cloth-supported plastic or contemporary-designed material for the contemporary stool. On the colonial stool, a gimp, or decorative trim is necessary to cover the upholstery tacks and the edge of the covering. Cambric, a thin black material, is applied to the bottom of the stool.

The only tools necessary for upholstering footstools are scissors and a magnetic tack hammer.

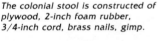

The colonial stool is constructed of plywood, 2-inch foam rubber, 3/4-inch cord, brass nails, gimp.

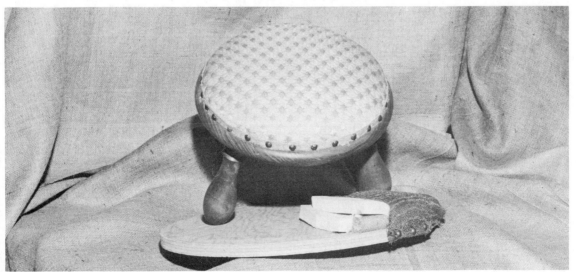

The Queen Anne stool has corner blocks to hold the seat, and is rabbeted.

Materials for the Queen Anne stool, showing 1/4-inch plywood, foam rubber, and covering.

CONSTRUCTION

The colonial footstool has a solid base of wood. Around this base, a 3/4-inch edge cord is tacked to build up the thickness of the seat and produce a rounded edge on the stool. If foam rubber is used, 1-inch thickness is placed inside the edge cord, and a second 1-inch piece is placed on top (cut flush with the outside edge of the cord). If horse hair or moss is used for filling, the rope edge should also be used and the filling should be about 3 inches thick, compressing to about 2 inches when the cover is applied.

With padding in place, carefully position the cover allowing about 2 inches extra on all sides. Start with four 3-ounce tacks, placing them across from each other. When the cover is held in place, put a tack between each of the four, being careful to pull the cover hard enough to avoid pleats or wrinkles. Repeat this tacking procedure until the tacks are about 3/4 inch apart around the entire stool.

A gimp is applied to hide the tacks and the edge of the covering. Gimp can be applied with gimp tacks or decorative upholstery nails placed about 1 inch apart. To add a professional touch, cambric can be applied to the bottom of the seat. When applying the cambric, cut about 1 inch larger than necessary so the edge can be turned under.

If needlepoint is to be applied, it must be "blocked" or made square by dipping it in water and tacking it on a piece of square plywood to dry. When dry, the same procedures are used as for other coverings.

The Queen Anne footstool has a removable plywood seat. A piece of 1/4-inch plywood is cut 5/16-inch smaller than the opening in the stool.

Glue 1-inch foam rubber on the plywood bottom, and trim flush with edge. Apply covering, being sure to center the pattern. If using a tapestry, be sure the pattern is straight. Pull the covering around and tack on the bottom of the seat. Place one tack on the middle of each side, then work toward the corners.

After excess cover is trimmed, tack the cambric on using the same procedure as the colonial stool. The finished seat is fastened to the frame with screws through the braces in the corners of the stool. A rabbet should always be made around the edge so the seat can fit below the wooden edge, and produce a tight edge around the stool.

To cover the contemporary footstool, glue 3 inches of foam rubber on a piece of 3/4-inch plywood cut to correct seat size. Drill four air holes, 3/8 inch in diameter, in the plywood bottom. Place the cover on the seat with about 2 inches added to each side for pulling the material. The covering must be pulled hard enough to round the top edge of the foam rubber to a 2-inch radius.

On each corner, a pleat must be made by cutting out the excess material and stretching the cover around the end. Make two pleats on each end so the front and back edges of the stool are smooth. The material will be tacked on the bottom, as in the Queen Anne stool. The cambric is then applied.

You can add a professional touch by using 3/4-inch cord on all edges if the cover is to be tacked on the edge as in the colonial stool. Pull the cover with equal pressure on all sides.

32: Table with Mosaic Inlay

The tile inlay on this piece makes it truly a work of art. And the procedure is not difficult. This project allows you to gain more experience with both hand and power tools.

* * *

This table was built from Costa Rican mahogany; however, any good cabinet wood such as walnut, Philippine mahogany, or cherry would be as satisfactory.

The construction is simple. The base is a bandsawed disc with a fancy edge applied with a router. Four feet are glued to the underside of this base. The spindle is turned from a glued-up piece. If 2-inch stock is available, however, it will not be necessary to glue material for the spindle. Be sure to make the pegs on each end of the spindle a tight fit in the base and in the top (Fig. 2). The spindle peg fits into a 1 1/2-inch hole in the bracket that is screwed to the underside of the top. Refer to the third figure for these operations.

A table with mosaic tile insert like the one shown here offers the chance to use both hand and power tools.

122

The top is a glue-up of several pieces to make one 14-inch square piece. Be careful to select boards of matching grain and color. Run a fancy edge on the top with a router or shaper. Then mount the top on a faceplate on the outboard end of the lathe. Run at slowest speed to carefully cut the groove for the mosaic tile. Cut this groove about 1/8 inch wider than the tile so there is grout space on all sides of the tiles. The depth of the groove should be such that the surface of the finished tile is slightly above the wood surface.

The tiles are cemented in place with mosaic-tile cement. Place the tile carefully in the groove, being sure to space them evenly. The grouting is done next, using mosaic-tile grout. Mask the tabletop with newspaper and masking tape to keep the grout off the wood. Work the grout into the open spaces between the tile. After it has dried for a few minutes, wipe off the excess with a dry rag and polish the surface of each tile. Smooth and shape the grout lines with your finger or a pencil eraser. Refer to the fourth figure.

Use a teak stain, followed with a Danish-type oil finish. While the finish is still wet, sand with 500-grit wet or dry paper. This produces a very smooth surface and fills the pores. Finally, apply several coats of paste wax.

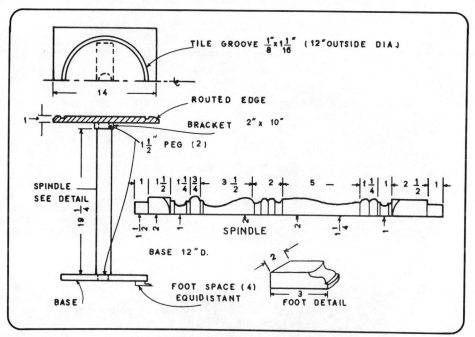

Parts and dimensions for mosaic table.

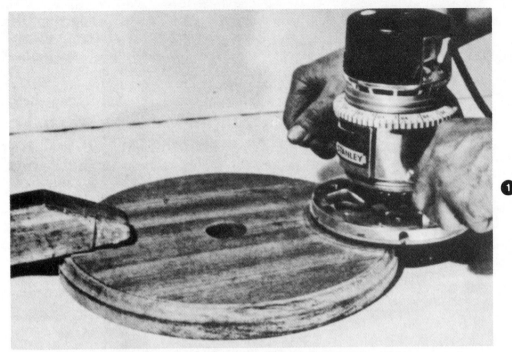

1) A portable router is used to put a fancy edge of the table base as well as the tabletop.

2) Both ends of the spindle are attached with 1 1/2-inch peg, fitted in a test block.

3) A flat turning chisel or skew is used to cut the tile groove on the tabletop.

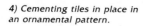

4) Cementing tiles in place in an ornamental pattern.

4

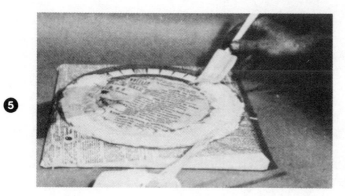

5

5) Grouting tile-work after tabletop has been carefully masked.

33: Wood and Metal

Are you ready for something different? How about putting wood and metal together in the same project? The combinations are unlimited, and perhaps working with metal will open up a whole new area of craftsmanship interest.

* * *

Contact cements[1] opened up many new horizons for craftsmen. In projects such as this one, these comments join two different materials rigidly and permanently.

Spun-metal bases for bowls, trays, and wood serving plates are attractive. Wood bases for metal dishes and bowls are equally attractive. You begin by following customary turning procedures for the bowl.

Variations of wood and metal bowls.

PROCEDURE

Bandsaw or jigsaw the blank for turning. Mount the faceplate on what will be the top of the bowl. Turn the back to shape. Carefully make the bottom flat. This is important so that there will be sufficient surface contact for good adhesion in the cementing process.

After the bottom is finished, mount the faceplate on it. Next, dish out the top side of the bowl using a roundnose turning chisel. Sand and finish the bowl as desired. The bottom surface, on which the contact cement will be applied, should be left unfinished.

The spun-metal base will not present any problems to the experienced metal spinner, and only a few to the beginner.

Spinning should be done only on a metal-turning lathe, or a good, sturdy wood-turning lathe equipped with thrust bearings on the headstock. It is preferable to have a ball-bearing tailstock center.

The spinning setup that we used can be seen in the accompanying strip of photographs. The tool rest is homemade and can be adapted to your lathe. The wood chuck can be turned from a hard, close-grained wood such as maple or birch. The metal blank is held against it by the pressure from the tailstock center against a follow block. The follow block is approximately 1/4 inch smaller in diameter than the base diameter of the chuck.

The metal blank should be lubricated with beeswax, tallow, soap, or stick wax. The metal is forced to the chuck gradually. Too much pressure will cause buckling and wrinkling.

Forming the metal causes it to harden and it is necessary to soften it by annealing. For copper and brass, the annealing can be done by heating it to a dull red and allowing it to cool by itself, cleaning off the oxide in an acid bath, and washing the metal in clear water. The spinning can then be continued. A deep spinning will require several annealings.

It is wise to trim the edge periodically during the spinning operation. This helps to keep the metal round. If the metal should be moved too much between annealings, it might wrinkle. Wrinkles can be removed easily by shaping it with a mallet over a stake. Wrinkles can also be removed on the lathe by using a back stick. Both methods work equally well, once the metal has been annealed.

When the spinning is completed, remove the scratches from the metal with emery cloth and oil, or aluminum oxide paper and water. Follow this operation with a rubbing, using fine steel wool and oil. Next, buff the metal with Tripoli polishing compound; wash it in hot, soapy water, and dry it.

You can oxidize the metal before you lacquer, if you wish.

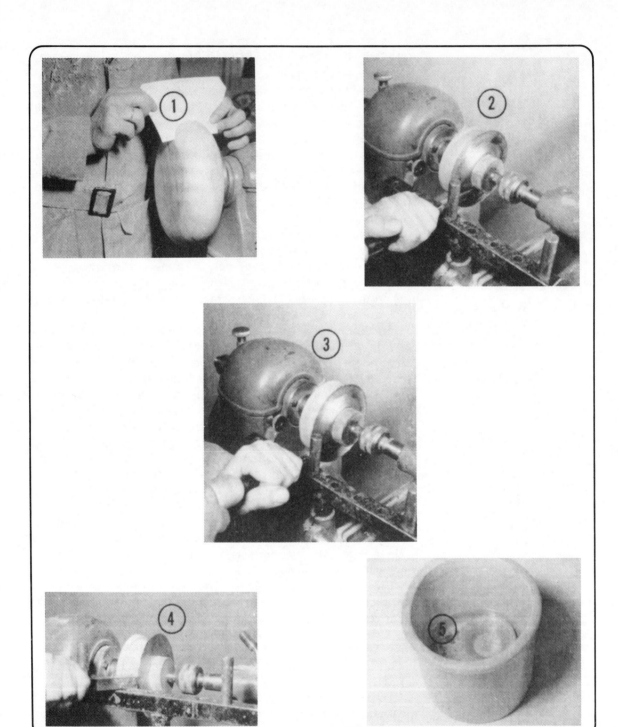

Tricks that will help in making a wood/metal project: 1) Check the outside contour of the wooden part with a template. 2) Try to prevent the metal from belling back towards the turning tool. 3) When setting the metal to chuck, start shaping it from the bottom to firmly anchor it in place. 4) During the metal spinning, periodically trim the circumference. 5) Use one part sulfuric acid to ten parts water to remove oxide formed during annealing. (Caution: Add acid to water.)

A variety of colors—ranging from browns to blues to black—are possible with chemicals. One of the easiest chemicals to work with is potassium sulfide (K_2S). A warm solution of this chemical will impart the colors to the metal.

To fasten the parts together, follow the manufacturer's directions for using the contact cement. Apply the cement generously to both parts. Allow it to dry until all stickiness has disappeared. Carefully align the parts to be fastened together. Place them together. Press firmly. That's all there is to it.

---

[1]Manufacturers of contact cements that have been used successfully are: Elmer's Contact Cement, Borden Co., New York, N.Y.; Formica Fast Dry Contact Bond Cement, Formica Company, Cincinnati, Ohio; Weldwood Contact Cement, United States Plywood Corporation, New York, N.Y.

Part Five

Finishes and Finishing

The finish—the final touches—makes a nice piece an outstanding one. The extra time and patience is worth the fine quality.

In this section we have broken down the finishing process into seven steps: preparing the wood, staining, sealing and filling, applying finish by brush, applying finish by spraying, use of penetrating oil finishes, and finally, French polishing on the wood lathe.

The finish in these exercises is applied not to a project, but to scrap pieces of wood. Such experimentation is advisable, especially to those woodworkers unfamiliar with finishes and finishing.

Preparing the Wood

For this first activity I used 4-x-11-inch panels of 1/4-inch un-finished plywood. Solid wood panels, most of which can be found in the "shorts" bin, can also be used. You will need several different open-grained hardwoods (oak, walnut, mahogany), close-grained hardwoods (maple, birch, willow, etc.) and softwoods (white pine, knotty pine, fir). Cut several panels of each species. This will allow you to apply different finishes to the same species. Cut at least one walnut panel with some light colored sap streak showing.

PROCEDURE

To prepare the wood for the finish, first remove smudges and dirt resulting from shipping and handling. A clean cloth moistened with turpentine or mineral spirits will remove most dirt. Any remaining dirt must be sanded off.

Dents caused during shipping or by clamps during gluing can be easily removed by putting a few drops of water on the dent. The water will swell the wood fibers back to their original shape. Large dents might require special treatment.

Make a pad of about four layers of clean cheesecloth. Wet the pad and squeeze out excess water but leave the pad saturated. Place the wet pad on the dent and apply a hot iron to the pad above the dent for five to 10 seconds. A hot soldering iron or household iron set on the *cotton* setting will work well. The water that has soaked into the wood will be turned into steam, which will push the mashed fibers back to their original shape. Deep dents may require several applications of heat before they can be raised. (Note: A *cut* in the wood cannot be corrected in this way.) Let the wood dry at least one hour before sanding.

SANDING

Most woodworkers have discovered, often after the stain or first coat of finish was applied, that scratches or blemishes seemed to appear out of nowhere. A scratch hardly noticeable and easily overlooked during sanding will be magnified by the finish. In extreme cases, an abrasive paper as coarse as 60 to 80 grit will be needed to remove the ridges. The use of a sanding block is a must. After the mill marks have been leveled using the coarse paper, proceed through several sandings using progressively finer paper. If you try to jump from a coarse to a fine abrasive, the larger stain-absorbing scratches will remain to mar the finish.

It is a chore to resand once you have started to apply the

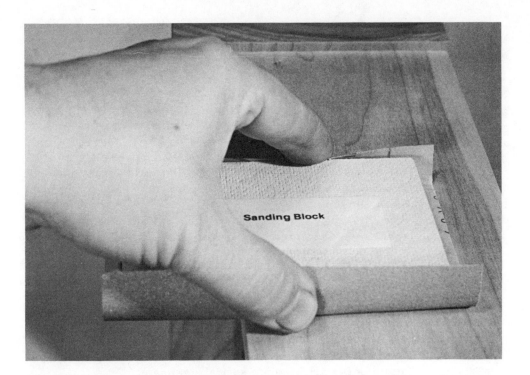

Sanding Block

When finishing, use a sanding block.

finish and difficult to completely hide the fact that some retouching had been done. So, sand carefully and thoroughly. This could be the most important step in the finishing process.

Careful sanding can eliminate several problems that often ruin a finish. One of the most common problems is the failure to remove marks left by woodworking machines, often called "mill marks." The jointer and planer leave small scallops or ridges similar to the surface of a washboard. These must be removed or a mottled, striped effect will appear when the stain is applied. Cross-grain sanding will cause scratches that soak up more stain than the surrounding wood. The scratches will always appear several shades darker than the rest of the finish. Always sand with the grain. Never sand across the grain.

Always do the final sanding by hand, using a sanding block on flat surfaces. Carefully sand with the grain using a 220 grit garnet paper. If defects have been removed and care has been taken in the use of progressively finer abrasive paper, then this final sanding will develop a fine "polished" surface that will absorb stain evenly and produce a high-quality finish.

FINISHING RECORD

A record of the steps in finishing each panel will add greatly to the future value of the panel as your own teaching aid. A "finishing record," such as the one below, can be typed on a half sheet of paper and glued to the back of each panel. The printed procedure can be followed when duplicating a finish.

Wood   _____

Stain   _____

Finish   _____

Schedule:

1.   _____
2.   _____
3.   _____
4.   _____
5.   _____
6.   _____
7.   _____
8.   _____
9.   _____

MATERIALS

The basic stock of finishing materials listed below will be used in the activities that follow. Use it to start a demonstration kit, which, when assembled and kept separate from the general stock, becomes a readily available source of supplies for teaching finishing.

- ☐ Stain, in assorted colors
- ☐ water (analine dye powder)
- ☐ oil
- ☐ gelled
- ☐ Shellac, 4-pound, cut, white
- ☐ Denatured alcohol (shellac thinner)
- ☐ Enamel, oil base
- ☐ Varnish, oil base
- ☐ Turpentine or mineral spirits
- ☐ Penetrating oil finish
- ☐ Wood filler, paste, natural
- ☐ Artists color in oil (raw umber, raw sienna, burnt umber, black)
- ☐ Lemon oil polish
- ☐ Sanding block
- ☐ Stir sticks
- ☐ Rubbing oil (mineral oil)
- ☐ Felt rubbing pads
- ☐ 000 steel wool pads
- ☐ 1-inch Bristle brushes

- ☐ Cheesecloth (make pads about 4-inches square—4 layers thick)
- ☐ Burlap (washed feed sacks and cut into 6-inch square pads)
- ☐ Garnet finishing paper 120, 180, 220 grit
- ☐ Silicon carbide wet-on-dry paper, 400 grit
- ☐ Paste floor wax
- ☐ Rottenstone powder
- ☐ Pumice powder
- ☐ Assorted cans for cleaning brushes and holding liquids

Staining

Wood is stained for several reasons. Often there is not an even color to a piece of wood. When several pieces are glued together there will often be a noticeable difference in the color of the pieces. This color difference must be evened out. Many people feel modern hardwoods are not as pretty as the woods cut and dried years ago. Stains can enhance the natural color of wood, adding an intensity and depth not found naturally. Staining will not make one wood look like another, for it does not change the grain pattern. Pine cannot be made to look like walnut regardless of the stain used. The grain patterns of the two woods are quite different and any knowledgeable woodworker will know the difference.

In this lesson you will apply stain to the panels prepared last time. Remove all dirt and dust. Number the panels or attach the finishing records to the backs of the panels. If the panels are to be used for display, the record sheets can be attached later.

Pigmented stain is recommended for use by students and novice woodworkers. Though the pigment tends to hide the grain and natural beauty of the wood, ease of application makes it a preferred stain. If a stain must be stirred or is a homogenized or gelled stain, it is a pigmented stain. The oil base stain is readily available and is recommended for use here.

Spread the stain uniformly over the panel using a good-quality bristle brush. Allow it to dry about five minutes and then wipe off with a clean rag or with a pad of cheesecloth. Turn the pad frequently to keep from wiping stain back onto the wood. Wipe with the grain to prevent streaking. Pigmented stains will accumulate in blemishes and corners and must be removed carefully and completely.

If a lighter shade is desired, wipe off the stain sooner. A second coat can be applied if a darker shade is desired.

The stain can also be wiped on using a pad of four or five layers of cheesecloth. Dip the pad into the stain and wipe onto the wood, carefully spreading it evenly. Intensity of color can be controlled by the amount of stain applied and wiped off. To produce a lighter shade, wipe off excess stain with a clean pad, allowing only a short time for the stain to soak into the wood. Many woodworkers feel it is easier to wipe the stains and, with students, the procedure eliminates the problem of cleaning brushes. Disposable plastic gloves should be worn when wiping on stains.

Stain the panels using different shades of stain for each species of wood. The fact that a stain is labeled "cherry" simply means that the manufacturer felt that was the shade cherry wood should be. You might prefer a different shade. Many people prefer cherry wood stained a lighter "fruitwood" rather than the dark red commonly seen. The collection of panels thus stained can be used later when selecting a finish for a woodworking project.

Prestraining is often necessary to cover blemishes or light colored areas such as the sap streaks often found in walnut. Water soluble dye stains can be put on the light areas only, giving the area a color similar to the rest of the piece. The entire piece can then be stained with pigmented stain in the normal manner.

Water soluble dye stain powders are mixed, using 1 ounce of powder to one pint of water. Mix thoroughly in a glass container until all the powder is dissolved. Apply to a piece of scrap wood to test for the desired color. If too dark, add water; if too light, add powder to the mixture. Repeat until the desired shade is obtained. Remember—stains dry several shades lighter than they appear when wet. It is always best to test a stain on a scrap piece of wood and let it dry before using on a piece of work.

End grain will soak up much more stain than edge or face grain, leaving an area that is much darker than the rest of the wood. This can be prevented by first wiping or brushing solvent into the end grain, followed immediately by an application of the stain. Use turpentine for oil stains, water for water-based stains, and denatured alcohol spirit for alcohol-based stains.

If, after staining, you discover mill marks, scratches from cross-grain sanding, or other blemishes, you will have to resand and then re-stain the panels. These blemishes will be magnified by the finish and will become more noticeable. Correct them *before* proceeding to the later finishing steps.

Most stains can be applied with a brush.

Sealing and Filling

The panels you have prepared in the first two parts must now be sealed to prevent the color of the stain from blending and bleeding into the finish coats to follow.

A wash coat (6 parts denatured alcohol to 1 part 4-pound cut white shellac) is recommended. The sealer must be made with a solvent different than that used in the stain or in the coats of finish to follow. The alcohol and shellac works well when oil or water-based stains and oil- or lacquer-based finishes are used.

Brush on the sealer uniformly and allow it to dry completely, overnight if possible. The wash coat will have a watery consistency and can be flowed on freely, but try to eliminate running.

It might be necessary to sand the dried sealer coat lightly. If the grain of the wood has been raised, minute wood fibers will be standing up like whiskers and must be sanded off. Use a 220 or 280 grit garnet finishing paper held lightly in your hand. Be careful not to sand through the stain on the edges of the panels.

Wipe off all sanding dust with a tack rag. A few drops of the shellac sealer on a pad of cheesecloth will make a good tack rag. Be sure the rag is only tacky; too much moisture can cause streaking. The tack rag can be stored in a tightly sealed jar and re-moistened with drops of shellac or warm water when needed.

Open-grained woods such as oak and walnut and some mahoganies must be filled before a smooth finish can be obtained. It is nearly impossible to get the finish to fill in the open pores of the wood and give a smooth finish.

Though colored fillers can be purchased, a natural (uncolored) filler can be colored to match the wood and stain. Artists colors in oil can be mixed with oil-based filler to give the desired shade; raw umber, raw sienna, and burnt sienna in different amounts produce shades of brown and red-brown. Black can be added to darken the color. Add only a few drops of color at a time to the thoroughly mixed filler. These colors are quite concentrated and a small amount goes a long way. The filler should be colored several shades darker than the stained wood. This helps accent the grain of the wood and bring out its beauty. The filler will dry to a lighter shade than it appears when wet, so it is best to test it on a piece of stained scrap wood before using.

When purchased, the filler will probably have settled out with a liquid on top and hard filling agent in the bottom. This must be mixed thoroughly before it can be colored and used. Some frequent stirring might also be necessary while the filler is being used.

Apply paste wood filler with a short bristle brush. Work the filler down into the pores of the wood, applying it to small areas

When the filler dries to a dull sheen, wipe off, against the grain, with clean burlap pads.

at a time. The filler can also be applied by wiping it on with the fingers. Wear a pair of disposable plastic gloves and work the filler into the wood forcing it down into the pores.

Allow the filler to dry until the gloss begins to disappear. Wipe off all excess filler with a pad of clean burlap. Wipe across the grain to remove the filler from the surface of the wood but not from the pores. You are trying to fill only the open pores, so carefully remove all excess filler. Next wipe lightly with the grain using a clean pad of cheesecloth. This will help clean the surface and smooth the surface of the filler.

Allow the filler to dry for at least 24 hours before applying a coat of sealer. This second sealer coat prevents the color in the filler from bleeding into the coats of finish, which will follow. Light sanding of the filler coat might be needed, again being careful not to cut through the edges of the panels.

At this point all of your panels should have been stained, sealed, and the open-grained woods filled and sealed a second time. You are now ready to begin applying the coats of finish.

Applying Finish by Brush

The panels are now ready for the application of the final coats of protective finish. In this installment you will use a brush to apply finish to approximately one-half of the prepared panels. The remaining panels will be put aside and finished in the next installment.

PREPARATION

Your work area must be well ventilated and free of dust. Varnishes are best applied when the temperature of the room and the varnish is above 70 degrees Fahrenheit. Do not try to apply varnish in a cold or humid atmosphere.

Most brushing finishes are slow drying and therefore a dust-free work area is necessary. Many woodworkers try to apply finish at the end of the work day so the finish can dry overnight without people moving around and stirring up dust. Try to suspend any machine work and sanding when finishing is being done. Clean the work area well, sweeping the floors with a sweeping compound and vacuuming dust from machines. With care, the finishing area can be kept relatively clean during finishing.

Varnish has been listed as the most satisfactory finish coat for the do-it-yourself woodworker. Varnish can be sprayed or brushed on. Where expensive spray equipment is not available, a high-quality finish can be achieved by brushing.

The solvents used in varnish are less volatile than in lacquers. The slower drying makes varnish easy to apply with satisfactory results. Good varnishes are resistant to water, alcohol, and most household liquids.

When selecting a varnish it is always best to get a high-quality material. Most varnishes formulated for use on fine furniture are "short oil" varnishes containing 5 to 12 gallons of oil per 100 pounds of resin. The short oil varnishes produce a hard finish that can be rubbed and polished to produce a high gloss of a lower luster satin finish. A good furniture varnish can be purchased as a "piano," "rubbing," or "polishing" varnish. Spar or floor varnish, though giving a good protective finish, will not produce the desired rubbed or polished finish.

When preparing the varnish, stir it gently with a clean stir stick. Do not shake the can. Doing so traps air bubbles in the liquid that will show up in the finish. A high-quality varnish should have nothing in it that needs to be mixed.

A high-quality bristle brush is best for applying varnish. When properly cared for, a quality brush will last a long time.

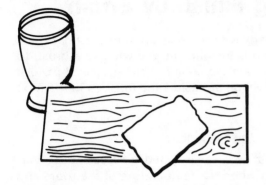

A tack rag can be stored in a jar and used many times to remove dust before applying a coat of finish.

Be careful that a synthetic bristle brush such as nylon is not used in a synthetic finish that will dissolve the bristles of the brush.

A new brush or one that has not been used in pigmented finishes is preferable. Once a brush has been used for applying a colored finish or stain, the coloring is nearly impossible to remove. The remaining color can bleed into the clear finish, leaving streaks or cloudiness.

The surface to be finished must be clean and free of dust and dirt. Remove all dust that might remain from sanding the sealer coat. Carefully wipe the piece with a tack rag to pick up any small particles of dust that might remain.

APPLYING VARNISH

For the test panels, a 1-inch bristle brush will work well. For larger work you might need larger brushes, as large as 3 inches for a table top.

With a clean work piece, a good brush, varnish, and a clean work area, you are now ready to apply the finish.

Dip the brush into the can of finish only about 1/3 of the way up on the bristles. Do not drag the brush over the edge of the can to remove excess finish. This will cause bubbles in the can of finish. Instead, light tap the brush on the inside side of the can above the finish. Excess finish will flow back into the can without forming bubbles.

If you are working from a large can of finish, pour the amount you think you will use into a clean container, and work out of this second container. Each time you dip the brush into the can there is a chance of carrying some dirt from the work piece to the can of finish. You should keep the original container free from dirt or coloring of the stain or filler.

Varnish is best applied by flowing it onto the surface in thin, even coats. Exact smoothness is not necessary because the slow-

142

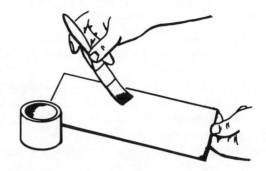

A light touch is needed when brushing on varnish. Use a 1-inch
bristle brush for small jobs.

drying finish will "flow out" smooth. Apply the varnish using a
light touch, bending the bristles only slightly and using as few
strokes as possible. Do not drag the brush over the edge of the
workpiece. This will drag extra finish out of the brush causing
runs down the side of the piece. Brush from the center toward
the edges.

Flow on the finish in one direction then go back over,
smoothing out at right angles to the original direction. Then go
back over with a light "feather touch," lightly dragging the tips
of the bristles over the wet finish to smooth it out and break any
bubbles that might have formed. Where possible, this last strok-
ing should be done in the direction of the grain of the wood.

It is best to start applying finish to the backs and undersides
of a workpiece. On a chair, for example, you should begin with
the bottom of the seat, then the legs. Turn the chair over and
apply finish to the back and then, finally, to the seat.

On vertical surfaces you must flow on smaller amounts of
finish on smaller areas to prevent running and sagging. On round
surfaces such as table and chair legs, apply the finish around the
round surface, then finish by smoothing out lengthwise. Be careful not to allow the varnish to build up in turnings or carvings.
Apply only a small amount of finish at a time. Allow varnish to
dry overnight. If drying conditions are not ideal, drying might
take longer.

To obtain a high-quality finish, at least two coats will be
needed with sanding between each. When each coat is dry, sand
lightly with 220 grit garnet paper. The final coat can be sanded
with 400 grit wet-to-dry paper lubricated with a small amount
of water. Steel wool (000) can be used for this final rubbing, but
be careful to remove all the small fibers that break off or they
can become embedded in the finish.

Applying Finish by Spraying

The advantage of spraying over brushing is ease of application. If proper procedures are followed an even, smooth coat of finishing material can be applied in a fraction of the time required for brush application. The faster drying materials, such as lacquer, can be sprayed, thus further shortening the time needed for the finishing operation. Several coats of a fast-drying finish can be sprayed in the time required for the application and drying of one coat of the slower drying brushing materials.

The procedures for preparing wood for spray finishing are essentially the same as those described in the previous article—applying the finish by hand—and will not be repeated here. If you have been following this series, working on practice panels, you should have about one-half of your panels finished by brushing. The remaining panels will now be finished by spraying.

The work area needed for spraying should be well lighted, well ventilated, and explosion-proof. The ventilation system, such as a spray booth, should include some method for removing the finishing materials from the air before exhausting. Waterfall and filter systems are the most common. The explosion-proof feature should not be overlooked or passed over lightly. Many finishing materials, especially lacquers, are explosive when atomized. Under the right conditions, even the smallest spark will ignite the vapors and cause an explosion. Most commercially made spray booths, when properly installed, will meet the necessary safety requirements.

Though knowledge of the various types of spraying equipment is important to successful spraying, limited space does not permit a detailed explanation here. Instead, the reader is referred to the many excellent books and publications available from manufacturers of spray equipment.

The correct air pressure for spraying varies for different types of finishing materials and the equipment being used. Normally the working pressure is in the range of 25 to 65 psi. Follow the manufacturer's recommendations to determine the proper pressure for your particular situation.

Some finishing materials can be sprayed straight from the container, while others must be thinned as much as half-and-half with the appropriate thinner. Again, the manufacturer's recommendations should be followed.

HOLDING AND MOVING THE GUN

The spray gun must be held perpendicular to the work surface as in first figure. The distance the gun is held from the sur-

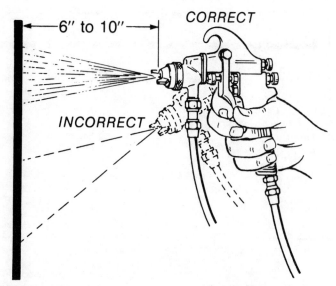

6" to 10"

CORRECT

INCORRECT

Hold gun perpendicular to surface being sprayed.

face and the speed it is moved are related. Most operators will move the gun in and out as needed for different jobs. A full wet coat of finishing material is needed. The amount of material applied can be controlled by the distance of the gun from the surface (closer, more finish applied; farther away, less material applied) and the speed the gun is moved (faster, less material applied; slower, more material applied). By balancing the two, a full wet coat can be applied without runs or sags or areas of too little material applied as in second figure.

TRIGGERING

The operator should learn to "trigger" the spray gun at the end of each stroke. Each stroke is begun off the edge of the work surface and ends off the opposite edge. The gun is triggered off at the end of the stroke and back on as the next stroke is begun in the opposite direction. If this "triggering" procedure is not followed, a build-up of finishing material along the edges of the workpiece can result, as in the third figure.

BANDING

Most spray gun operators use a banding technique. On large surfaces a single vertical stroke is sprayed along the edges to assure complete coverage. The horizontal strokes are begun at the top, spraying over the top edge slightly to assure complete coverage of the edge. Each succeeding horizontal stroke is lapped or "banded" at least 50 percent over the preceding stroke. This can be done consistently by aiming the center of the spray pattern at the lower edge of the preceding band as in third figure.

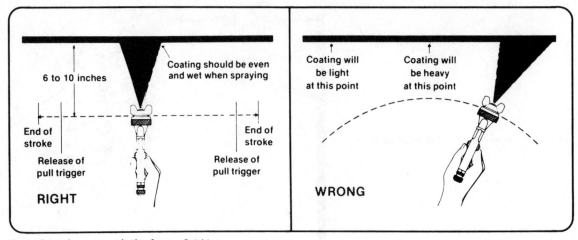

The right and wrong methods of spray finishing.

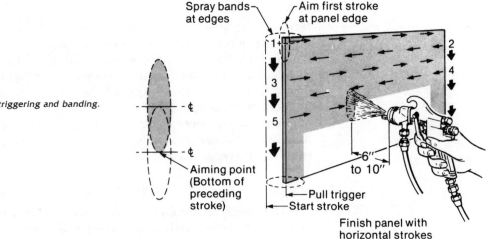

Spray finishing—triggering and banding.

COMMON PROBLEMS

Some problems may be encountered as you apply finish by spraying. Several of the most common and their causes are described here.

Orange Peel is a rough surface on the finish resembling the rind of an orange. This can be caused by using the wrong solvent when thinning the finishing material or by incorrect air pressure.

Runs or Sags are the result of the application of too much finishing material to a vertical surface. Holding the gun too close to the work or moving it too slowly over the work are the most common causes.

Pin Holes are often caused by water in the air lines being sprayed into the wet finish. Usually when this occurs, the oil and water extractor has accumulated a large amount of water and must be drained.

Practice is important for an inexperienced spray gun operator. Practice can be obtained by spraying onto sheets of brown wrapping (kraft) paper fastened to an easel or sheet of plywood propped up in the spray booth. The spray pattern will be easy to see because it shows up dark where it wets the surface of the paper. Once the students have learned the adjustment of the gun to get the proper spray pattern, the proper distance and movement of the gun over the work surface and the banding and triggering techniques, they are ready to work on their projects.

FINAL STEP

The application of a coat of paste wax is often the final step in finishing a piece of wood furniture. Though a clear paste floor wax can be used, many wood finishers prefer the darker waxes made specifically for use on furniture.

There is some controversy surrounding the use of wax on furniture. When applied too heavily or when many coats are applied over a long period of time, wax can build up, causing a gummy surface. Some waxes will water-spot and turn white from moisture or heat.

Lemon oil is considered by many to be the best furniture polish and wood preservative. It can be applied with a cloth as a furniture polish when dusting. It will not build up like wax and will help restore oils to the wood, preserving it and acting as a barrier to moisture.

On the panels you have finished in this series you can apply a light coating of paste wax or forego the wax and apply lemon oil. If you are in an experimental mood, treat several of the panels differently and observe any differences that might occur over a long period of time.

You are now ready to do the final rubbing or polishing on the finish. The next article will discuss penetrating finishes. If you have applied finish to all your test panels you might want to prepare several more panels for the application of penetrating finishes. Some of these could be stained, if desired.

Penetrating Oil Finishes

Oil finishes are among the oldest types of finishes. Some wood-workers feel they are among the best, particularly on the hard, close-grained woods. Walnut is particularly beautiful with an oil finish. A modern equivalent of these early finishes can be made with linseed oil cut with turpentine (2 parts commercial boiled linseed oil, 1 part pure turpentine). This finish must be rubbed vigorously with a hard finish cloth to bring out the luster. The vigorous rubbing develops heat from the friction, thus harden-ing the finish and giving the luster.

Several coats of the linseed oil finish must be applied. Some finishers recommend as few as five coats while others prefer as many as 20 coats. If no wax is put on top of the oil finish, new coats can be added whenever a renewed finish is desired.

Modern penetrating oils are replacing the older linseed oil finish. These newer materials soak into the wood and solidify deep below the surface, giving a deep protecting finish. The var-nishes and lacquers used in earlier parts of this series were sur-face finishes that gave a protection only on the surface of the wood.

APPLICATION

Most penetrating oil finishes can be applied on stained or unstained wood. If staining is desired, a sealer should *not* be used. The penetrating oil is its own sealer. The oil is flowed freely onto the wood with a brush, or it can be sprayed, applying a heavy coat. Allow the finish to soak into the wood. If, after a few minutes, the liquid has soaked into the wood in some areas and appears uneven, apply more finish to the areas where it has soaked in.

After about 15-20 minutes wipe off all finish remaining on the surface. A second coat can be applied at this time, again ad-ding more finish to areas where it is soaking in. Wipe off the ex-cess after about 15 minutes. If excess oil is allowed to remain on the wood too long, it could become sticky and not dry com-pletely. If this happens, flow a wet coat onto the sticky areas. This will soften the sticky materials, which then can be wiped off with a clean cloth. Polish the entire surface with a cloth to remove any remaining finishing materials. Let dry for about 12 hours and then polish to a soft luster.

You can apply an oil finish to several of the panels being fin-ished in this series. Try several different brands of finish. Watco Danish Oil finish, Minwax Antique Oil Finish and the Seal-A-Cell process should be tried. Though all are penetrating finishes, they will give slightly different final effects. All will give a finish that is low in luster, with little or no noticeable buildup of finish. This type of finish is often preferred on modern furniture, such as the Scandinavian styles.

Also apply the finishes to different woods. Walnut is often finished with oil finish—giving a deep, rich color without a heavy-appearing coating. Filler is not applied beneath oil finishes, so the open-grained woods will retain the porous look. On the harder, close-grained woods a smoother surface can be had.

The ease of application make the penetrating oil finishes particularly appealing. You can get a good-looking finish with a minimum of work, mess, and clean-up. On small projects, the penetrating finishes can be wiped on with a clean cloth, thus eliminating the need to clean brushes.

Oil finishes dry quickly and eliminate dust problems. Several light coats can be applied with a cloth without having to wait for the oil to soak in and then having to wipe off excess.

FINISHING SALAD BOWLS

I am often asked what finish is best for such items as wood bowls and cutting boards that come in contact with food. Though several quick answers are possible, the problem is not so easily or quickly solved. Several of the penetrating finishes are advertised as being non-toxic. While these may be safe for use on food utensils, I have developed some skepticism over the years. Some of the ingredients in the finish could be toxic. Some container labels warn against use of the piece until the finish has dried a specified period. I use only olive oil on salad bowls, cutting boards, and other wooden ware. These items need only a light coating to prevent the oils from the foods from soaking into the wood. These utensils should be cleaned only with a damp cloth. They should not be immersed in wash water or soaked. Cutting boards that receive heavy use should have several coats of oil applied, with more added periodically.

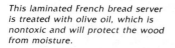
This laminated French bread server is treated with olive oil, which is nontoxic and will protect the wood from moisture.

French Polishing on the Wood Lathe

French polishing is a shellac finish applied with a cloth pad. The shellac is rubbed on by applying pressure to create heat, which dries the finish quickly. The shellac is usually thinned with denatured alcohol to give a thin polishing solution. Some finishers lubricate the pad with a small amount of light oil such as mineral oil or lemon oil. This makes the rubbing easier but does not retard the drying of the finish. Obviously, applying French polish to a large piece of furniture can be an arduous task. Considerable pressure is required to create the heat needed to dry the finish.

French polish has the advantages and disadvantages inherent in all shellac finishes. It has a tendency to turn milky white when subjected to moisture or water. It is also subject to damage by heat and has some tendency to check because of its elasticity.

French polishing is an excellent finish in some applications. The finish is beautiful because it is a thin and transparent coating that does not hide the grain of the wood. There is virtually no discoloration when white shellac is used, thus retaining the natural color of the wood.

Though any finish can be applied to lathe turnings, French polishing offers a particularly fast, easy, and beautiful finish. Many turnings such as lamps, candle sticks, and gavels can be finished while the piece is still in the lathe, thus speeding up the finishing process.

PREPARATION

Sand the turning with the lathe running at the slowest speed. Be careful how the paper is held. If your fingers are pressing hard against the work, heat from the friction will build up enough to burn you. This sanding will leave scratches in the work that go around the piece. You must stop the lathe, and maybe even remove the work to carefully sand away all these scratches by sanding in the direction of the grain. If these sanding marks are not removed, they will be magnified by the finish.

APPLICATION

The materials needed are white shellac (4-pound cut), denatured alcohol (shellac thinner), powdered pumice stone, mineral oil, and a soft cloth such as cheese cloth, folded into a pad.

Be certain the ends and edges of the pad are folded under and there are no loose ends or strings that can be caught in the turning piece of wood. A pad of 4 or 5 layers should be sufficient. The pad should be refolded or turned so that a new sur-

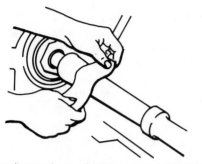

When sanding on the wood lathe, a strip of abrasive paper works well to prevent burning your fingers.

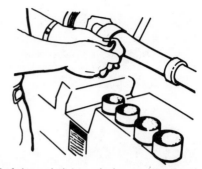

A pad of cheesecloth is used when applying French polish. Be certain there are no loose strings to catch in the spinning work.

face is used each time the finish is applied. Dried finish in the pad could scratch the work, especially if a second coating is being applied.

The lathe should be running at the slowest speed. The tool rest and tool post should be removed to prevent your hand from being pulled in between the work and the tool rest.

Dab the pad into the shellac, wetting the pad in a spot about the size of a half dollar. Touch this spot into the alcohol, to thin the shellac slightly. Drop several drops of the oil onto this area to serve as a lubricant. This can be done by dipping one or two fingers into the oil and letting the oil drop onto the wet spot of the pad. If you dip into the oil as you did with the shellac and alcohol, too much oil could be picked up.

Hold the wet spot of the pad against the turning piece of work. Apply pressure to create friction heat. Some judgment will have to be used here to apply enough pressure to create the needed heat but not creating enough heat to burn your fingers. It will take only a few seconds to dry the finish. When an area has been finished, pick up more shellac, alcohol, and oil in the pad and start another area, slightly overlapping the previously finished area.

A convenient way of handling the various finishing materials is to put each in a small container such as a small tuna can or metal cap from an aerosol can. These can be placed on the bed of the lathe in front of the work. It is easy to then dab the pad into each of the cans of materials as needed.

Powdered pumice stone can be used as a filler on some open-grained woods. A small amount of the pumice powder can be added to the pad each time finish is applied to the work. This needs to be done only on the first coat. Additional coatings can be applied without filler once the pores have been filled. On dark woods such as walnut, the white pumice powder may show white in the pores of the wood. Test this on a trial piece before applying it to a critical turning.

Index

Edited by Cherie R. Blazer

Other Bestsellers From TAB

☐ **66 FAMILY HANDYMAN®WOOD PROJECTS**

Here are 66 practical, imaginative, and decorative projects . . . literally something for every home and every woodworking skill level from novice to advance cabinet-maker: room dividers, a free-standing corner bench, china/book cabinet, coffee table, desk and storage units, a built-in sewing center, even your own Shaker furniture reproductions! 210 pp., 306 illus. 7″ × 10″.

Paper $14.95   **Hard $21.95**
Book No. 2832

☐ **79 FURNITURE PROJECTS FOR EVERY ROOM—Blandford**

Just imagine your entire home filled with beautiful, hand-crafted furniture! Elegant chairs, tables, and sofas, a hand-finished corner cupboard, luxurious beds and chests, and more! With the hands-on instructions and step-by-step project plans included here, you'll be ale to build beautiful furniture for any room . . . or every room in your home . . . at a fraction of the store-bought cost! 384 pp., 292 illus. 7″ × 10″.

Paper $16.95   **Hard $24.95**
Book No. 2704

☐ **PLANNING AND BUILDING FENCES AND GATES—AAVIM**

This colorfully illustrated guide gives you all the expert, step-by-step guidelines and instructions you need to plan and build durable, cost-effective fences and gates. You will be able to design and construct just about any kind of fence you can think of—barbed wire, woven wire, cable wire, mesh wire, board fences, electric fences, gates, and much more! 192 pp., 356 illus. 8 1/2″ × 11″. 2-Color Throughout.

Paper $14.95   **Book No. 2643**

☐ **UPHOLSTERY TECHNIQUES ILLUSTRATED—Gheen**

Here's an easy-to-follow, step-by-step guide to modern upholstery techniques that covers everything from stripping off old covers and padding to restoring and installing new foundations, stuffing, cushions, and covers. All the most up-to-date pro techniques are included along with lots of time- and money-saving, "tricks-of-the-trade" not usually shared by professional upholsterers. 352 pp., 549 illus. 7″ × 10″.

Paper $16.95   **Book No. 2602**

☐ **77 ONE-WEEKEND WOODWORKING PROJECTS—Percy W. Blandford**

Let this guide put the fun back into your hobby! Over-flowing with step-by-step instructions, easy-to-follow illus-trations, dimensioned drawings, and material lists, this indispensable guide includes plans for 77 projects: tables, racks and shelves, a take-down book rack, corner shelves, a vase stand, beds and cabinets, yard and garden projects, toys, games and puzzles, tools, and more. 304 pp., 226 illus.

Paper $14.95   **Hard $23.95**
Book No. 2774

☐ **THE FRUGAL WOODWORKER—Rick Liftig**

Who says you need an elaborate workshop to fully en-joy your woodworking hobby? And who says you have to spend a small fortune on expensive materials to produce pro-quality furniture? *Certainly not Rick Liftig*! And neither will you after you get a look at the expert advice, money-saving tips, and practical low-cost projects included in his exciting new woodworking guide: *The Frugal Woodworker*! You'll find invaluable advice on where and how to acquire wood at bargain prices, even for free! 240 pp., 188 illus.

Paper $12.95   **Hard $22.95**
Book No. 2702

☐ **A MASTER CARVER'S LEGACY—essentials of wood carving techniques—Bouche'**

All the step-by-step techniques for making a whole range of woodcarved items—gifts, accessories, furniture, toys, tools, utensils, and more—are included in this invaluable guide! Using the professional tips and techniques revealed by wood carving expert Brieuc Bouché, you can add hand-crafted furniture and accessories to your home that will be admired by all your family and friends. 176 pp., 135 illus. 8 1/2″ × 11″.

Hard $24.95   **Book No. 2629**

☐ **CABINETS AND VANITIES—A BUILDER'S HANDBOOK—Godley**

Here in easy-to-follow, step-by-step detail is everything you need to know to design, build, and install your own cus-tomized kitchen cabinets and bathroom vanities and cabi-nets for a fraction of the price charged by professional cabinetmakers or kitchen remodelers . . . and for less than a third of what you'd spend for the most cheaply made ready-made cabinets and vanities! 142 pp., 126 illus. 7″ × 10″.

Paper $12.95   **Book No. 1982**

*Prices subject to change without notice.

Look for these and other TAB books at your local bookstore.

TAB BOOKS Inc.
P.O. Box 40
Blue Ridge Summit, PA 17214

Send for FREE TAB catalog describing over 1200 current titles in print.
OR ORDER TOLL-FREE TODAY: **1-800-233-1128**